The Roots of Addiction

From Drug to Feelings, the Common Mechanism to know before treating one of the most widespread Disease

By

Emil Howthorn

The information herein is offered for informational purposes solely, and is universal as so. The presentation of the information is without contract or any type of guarantee assurance.

The trademarks that are used are without any consent, and the publication of the trademark is without permission or backing by the trademark owner. All trademarks and brands within this book are for clarifying purposes only and are the owned by the owners themselves, not affiliated with this document.

Table of Contents

Introduction

The word ' addiction' has become one of the phenomena or situations most common in our lives. But do we know precisely what that means or where did it originate?

Your child or your loved one in his life has faced a problem.

He was not able to solve the problem, so that created confusion for him. This could have been everything. It might be nervousness, or worries about school, or about a specific person who gave him trouble. It might even be the pain arising from an accident or procedure for which prescription drugs were administered lawfully and appropriately.

They were taking a drug to relieve the burden of the stress and the problem. For a while, the medication caused the problem to "go down." But after the medication wore off, they wanted more to keep the issue "solved." Eventually, for many of their problems, narcotics became the "solution." And as drug tolerance grew, it took more and more drugs to get the same "release" sensation, which is why a person can become emotionally addicted to drugs that are not physically addictive. What's more, though, a physical dependence sets in.

Addiction is a complex disease, often of a chronic nature that affects the brain and body functioning. It also causes serious harm to communities, households, relationships, schools, workplaces. The most common symptoms of addiction are extreme loss of control, persistent use despite severe consequences, guilt for use, unsuccessful quit attempts, resistance, and withdrawal.

Addiction is marked by the failure to stop drinking or taking alcohol, although it creates problems in your life using it. With negative consequences, this compulsive substance use is the result of changes in brain function and structure that influence the habits and behaviors of thought.

The neurotransmitter dopamine is released into the brain when you use drugs or alcohol, causing feelings of pleasure. The brain's memory area tracks this feeling's history. The learning center creates associations that are known as stimuli between the enjoyment, substance use, and environmental signs present during use.

Over time, the brain's link between use and the enjoyment it provides becomes stronger and can lead to severe cravings. The same mechanisms are producing these powerful cravings that drive us to eat food and procreate to survive. Addiction-related changes in brain function and structure are affecting the way we think and act.

That is why justifying your use of drugs is so easy. Excuses are easy to make on your own. And it's easy to do things like being dishonest or stealing, that you would never have done before you became addicted.

Most people see addiction as a question of personal weakness, started for self-gratification, and continued because of a lack of willingness or motivation to avoid it. Nevertheless, the idea that pleasure-seeking primarily induces addiction has fallen by the wayside within the medical and scientific community.

Clinicians and scientists alike now believe that many people engage in potentially addictive activities to escape both physical and emotional discomfort. People typically indulge in psychoactive activities that will make them feel good and feel better. The roots of addiction reside in activities related to the search for sensation and self-medication.

Drug and alcohol use can escalate rapidly or gradually to a condition based on individual risk factors of a person, as well as the type of drug he or she uses.

Those with addictive disorders may be aware of their addiction, but they may not be able to stop it if they so wish. The habit can cause health problems as well as issues with family members and friends at work. Drug and alcohol abuse is the number one cause of preventable diseases and premature death.

Addiction is not only limited to drugs or alcohol, but is also distributed through the social network, internet, video games, and even gambling ways.

Chronic stress, a history of abuse, mental illness, and a family history of addictions are the most common causes of addiction. Learning how these can lead to violence and addiction to addictive drugs can help you reduce the risk of becoming addicted.

Here, we're going to discuss addiction and its origins, and we're going to look at practical, useful ways to reduce the chance of becoming addicted.

Chapter 1: Etiology, psychology and human beings

Etiology applies to the conditions or triggers blamed for or related to the development of diseases. Mental and psychological problems are caused by internal factors, loss, discomfort, environmental factors, etc. and these factors must be understood in their significance and balance.

Psychological disorders are largely multi-factorial etiologies, which include complex interactions between genetic and environmental factors. Psychological etiology is about scientific research into the causes of a disease that cannot be scientifically explained. Etiology is made more difficult by the fact that most conditions have more than one purpose.

The biological processes which cause addiction involve brain reward pathways. Addictive behaviors share important neurobiological features: they include reward and reinforcement brain mechanisms that include dopamine from the neurotransmitter.

When researchers first began researching what caused addictive behavior in the 1930s, people who developed addictions assumed they were somehow morally flawed or deficient in willpower. They thought that overcoming addiction involved punishing miscreants or, in turn, encouraging them to muster the will to break a habit.

Addiction of any kind affects not only human beings but particularly the environment. Likewise, when a woman bears an infant and a new life grows within her, both environmental and physical factors affect the baby directly in the womb of the mother.

Pregnancy should be a time of excitement and empowerment in a woman's life. Sadly, a woman's safety and security may be affected by alcohol and mental health issues.

Let's get into the etiology and its psychological factors in depth.

1.1 Expounding the concept of Etiology

Did you figure out the trigger the last time your machine showed you a blue screen of death? All right, maybe you're not a professional computer. Come on with this one? Did you figure out the last time you blew a tire on your car, whether it was a stone, sharp rock, or something else that caused it or not?

Much like when you're searching for a flat tire's origin, doctors and scientists are trying to figure out the source of a person's disease similarly. Once they know the cause, they will treat the cause and do more to relieve their symptoms for the patient. Keep that in mind, when we explore disease etiology and go over some examples of this definition.

When a doctor tries to figure out the cause of an illness, they are merely trying to figure out the disease's etiology. Etiology is the cause of an illness or the research concerned with such purposes. The term etiology originates from the Greek etio-, meaning' causation' and -ology, referring to the scientific study of something. Since causes are always relative to their effects, the identification of etiological factors or causes of the disease requires the specification of some unusual disease trait.

Etiology of a disease, or cause, usually falls into three main categories: intrinsic, extrinsic, and idiopathic.

We'll think about etiologies intrinsic to you. Inherent means that have come from within. As a consequence of inherent causes, any pathological, or disease-causing, alteration that has arisen from within the body has occurred.

The following are examples of intrinsic factors:

• Hereditary conditions, or conditions that your parents pass on to you. Hemophilia is one example of this, a condition that leads to excessive bleeding.

• Diseases of metabolic and endocrine, or of the hormone. These are chemical signaling disorders and body activity. Diabetes mellitus, for example, is an endocrine disorder that causes high blood sugar.

• Neoplastic or cancer conditions where the body's cells develop out of control;

• Immune problems, such as allergies, which are immune system overreactions.

The second category of etiology for the disease is extrinsic etiologies. This means that the cause of the illness, or pathological change, originated outside the body.

Definitions of extrinsic factors are as follows:

• Infectious agents such as bacteria, viruses, fungi, and parasites

• Animal bites or stings

• Chemicals, heat, and radiation

• Iatrogenic causes: This is just an excellent way to say that the problem arose from the acts of a medical professional or within a medical setting.

Idiopathic etiologies are the third category of disease etiology: Of an unknown cause. Any disease of unclear or unknown origin may be considered idiopathic. For example, acute idiopathic polyneuritis, diffuse idiopathic skeletal hyperostosis, idiopathic pulmonary fibrosis, idiopathic scoliosis, and so on. The definition of etiology is further used in the study of causes and triggers that lead to the development of disease in drug use.

Etiological research seeks to classify the likely causes of drug use and its effects. There are several factors identified which contribute to the development of a substance use disorder. No consideration, however, or any group of elements can similarly influence all individuals or fully explain substance use.

Etiological research focuses primarily on the probable causes and correlates of drug use; it has identified many factors that affect drug use, though no single variable or set of variables explains an individual's use of drugs. There's just no cause to believe that all persons will be influenced in the same way by the same purpose, nor is there any reason to believe that the factors responsible for initiating substance use are of equal importance in continuing or increasing use.

One of the etiological research priorities has been to define variables (such as risk and protective factors) that may be correlated with the use of drugs. The fundamental interest in such variables is to assess whether risk management and protective factors can mitigate outcomes in drug use. Nonetheless, for targeted intervention measures to be either a risk factor or a protective factor, it is first necessary to show that the variable is adaptive and can be affected by environmental adjustments, or through educational or medical treatments.

1.2 Etiology and psychology

Psychology put is a discipline devoted to understanding human behavior. Psychologists are concerned with improving people's quality of life and their satisfaction with life. Psychologists find practices that promote adaptive actions for people's well-being and life satisfaction. Behaviors that help to impair the functioning of individuals and that life satisfaction are considered maladaptive behaviors. Psychological models are constructive for understanding why people participate in this unhealthy behavior since addiction is negative, maladaptive behavior.

Psychological etiology is about scientific research into the nature of a disease that cannot be scientifically explained. Etiology is made more difficult by the fact that most conditions have more than one cause.

The Freudian and post-Freudian psychoanalytic views were early etiologic theories. Sigmund Freud attributed deep-seated or secret unconscious impulses to emotional or neurotic conditions. Under Freud's approach, the unconscious played the primary role. The person in conflict, Freud says, he did not know the origin, because it was too deeply embedded in an obscure part of the mind. Freud postulated that a defense mechanism caused this burial into the unconscious had been enforced by the occurrence of previous traumas, inappropriate thoughts, or wanton drives. An individual can push these unsavory thoughts and memories as far away as possible from the conscious mind as a means of survival.

According to Freud, adolescence was the time when many repressed impulses and defense mechanisms started to flourish. In control of their own lives, children have no way of resolving feelings such as anger, fear, or remorse. Mostly, these feelings build up as the child's personality grows into adulthood. Any psychological condition from sexual dysfunction to anxiety could be explained by learning about a person's repressed feelings from childhood on.

Another kind of etiology that arose after Freud is called the etiology of behavior. It focuses on the habits identified as symptoms of mental disorders. Ivan Pavlov B. F. Skinner is two well-known behavioral psychologists. Behaviorists argue that action can be "educated" in different ways to respond to stimuli. A conditioned response is one that is acquired when a stimulus creates a reaction and somehow reinforces that response. For example, a young girl is told she's cute for screaming at a spider's sight. She discovers that onlookers respond favorably to this screech. This acquired behavior can develop over time into a genuinely paralyzing addiction for spiders. Behaviorists claim that just as a person may be conditioned in a specific way to respond to a stimulus, that same person may be conditioned to respond differently. In other words, it is possible to learn more appropriate behavior, which is the basis for conduct therapy.

While psychologists focused on the mind itself as the place where psychological impairment could begin, physicians and researchers continued to understand the biology that could influence mental disorders. Many of these studies have resulted in the refinement of prescription medicines which alter the biochemistry of a person to prevent or regulate various diseases such as depression or schizophrenia. Neuropathology may also act as a biological cause of psychological disorders or damage to brain tissue. Genetic research was conducted to determine causes at the DNA level for specific diseases. For decades, researchers have been trying to identify a gene that produces the schizophrenia "program." Reports of fully recovered schizophrenics treated without medication reportedly continued to increase by 2000. Psychological therapy for schizophrenic episodes seems to be just as successful as medical treatment.

The awareness of its possible causes is essential to the treatment of any condition. Before they can change behavior, psychologists must assess the etiology of a disease.

Psychological disorders often referred to as mental disorders, are cerebral anomalies which result in persistent patterns of behavior that can severely affect your daily function and life.

Several different psychological conditions were described and categorized, including eating disorders such as anorexia nervosa, mood disorders such as depression, personality disorders such as antisocial personality disorder; psychotic disorders such as schizophrenia; sexual disorders such as sexual dysfunction; and others. One individual may have several psychological disorders.

There are no known clear causes of psychological disorders, although contributing factors may include chemical brain imbalances, childhood experiences, heredity, infections, prenatal exposures, and stress. Many conditions happen more frequently in women, such as borderline personality and depression. Others are more common in men, including intermittent explosive disorder and substance abuse. Still, other illnesses, such as bipolar disorder and schizophrenia, affect approximately equal proportions of men and women.

When a person experiences long-term mood or cognitive problems or behavioral problems, a psychological assessment may be helpful, and a diagnosis of a mental disorder may follow. Treatment also requires psychotherapy to focus on behaviors, improvement of skills, and method of thinking. A person may be hospitalized for medical problems coexisting with each other, serious complications, extreme disorders, or substance abuse. For some psychiatric conditions, medications can be quite useful.

Those who have psychological disorders often get better when treated; however, relapses are likely. Many psychological problems, left untreated, can contribute to academic, legal, social, and job problems. Certain possible complications include alcohol poisoning, drug overdose, suicide, and violent behavior.

Psychologists say multiple possible reasons for addiction. Next, because of an abnormality, or "psychopathology," which presents itself as a mental illness, people can participate in dangerous behaviors. Second, people can learn to respond to their environment with unhealthy behavior. Fourth, the thoughts and beliefs of the people create their sensations. This, in effect, dictates their actions. As far as somebody's views and opinions are irrational or unhealthy, their efforts will be influenced equally.

The concept of psychopathology views mental disorders as the cause of addiction. Such complications could include cognitive problems, mood disorders, and other mental illnesses. Addiction and other mental health disorders (called co-morbidity) commonly occur together. Around half of the people seeking treatment for alcohol will also have another significant mental illness.

The definition of an addictive personality is linked to Psychopathology. The underlying factors in all addictive disorders could be other personality traits. These may include ignoring obvious problems, emotional regulation issues, and impulse management issues. There is no evidence to suggest an addictive personality as such. Nevertheless, addiction most frequently co-occurs with a class of disorders that are called Personality Disorders.

Most human behavior is an acquired behavior. That is also true of addictive behavior. Psychological research has helped us understand how people learn to participate in an activity that is unhealthy. This work, more significantly, allows us to know how people can unlearn a pattern.

Another psychological source of addiction is the minds and values of individuals. This is because our thoughts and beliefs are the basis of much of our behavior. It covers addictive behaviors. For example, if someone thinks redemption is not feasible, they're doubtful to make any attempt to leave. Psychologists have developed strategies for helping people change their beliefs and emotions. Afterward, their thoughts and attitudes always shift.

Psychology has also helped us understand when it's so difficult for people to avoid unhealthy behavior like drug use. People may find it difficult to recover because they lack excellent problem-solving skills and enough motivation. Drug addiction can also arise as a way to deal with painful or anxious feelings. Psychotherapy can help to reinforce people's motivation, and develop their problem-solving skills, ability to reduce stress and coping skills.

Addiction is such a complicated issue, that even after a century of discussion and progress in science and medicine, the problem of what causes it and what constitutes it remains somewhat unsettled. The psychology behind addiction covers many bases: whether it is an illness or a personal failure, the effect of lifestyle and childhood; family history and socioeconomic demographics; and the dozens of other factors that cannot be accounted for or measured.

1.3 Environmental factors and Social factors

Those involved in or dealing with addiction will be curious about how someone ends up with alcohol, substance, sex, or food addiction. Is it caused by something like genetics within a person, or something outside like the way a person is raised or with whom they hang out? Is it a product of childhood trauma, or are there moral factors?

Tens of billions of glial cells and neurons communicate to support us to think, sound, interpret, learn, and act in incredibly nuanced ways. Recent advances in neuroimaging, Opto-and chemogenetics, genetics, epigenetics, and other scientific techniques revolutionize our understanding of brain and brain disorders, covering molecules, cells, networks, processes, and individual and social behaviors.

Across the past several decades, there have been several studies investigating the causes of people's tendency to become addicted, and researchers have also attempted to determine the amount, significance and function of each person and environmental factor.

Researchers have been looking for the roots of addiction for years. If we could determine precisely what it is, that makes people susceptible to addiction— whether it's a biological or genetic trait, social factors, one's environment, some combination of these factors, or even something else altogether — we could potentially divert addiction development and cure those who have become chemically dependent.

There's particular excitement surrounding the genetic piece of the puzzle with the advanced technologies available today. But with addiction being such a big issue in all demographics, maybe it's time to turn our attention back to the community.

Most people engage in unhealthy alcohol and drug use, and anyone can develop a problem with the substance. Many people can develop severe addiction and make progress. Alcohol and drug use affects all, regardless of their age, gender, sex, ethnicity, or economic position. A large number of drug- and alcohol users -including many who frequently or extensively use them-do not develop addiction disorder.

As with other diseases, there are risk factors associated with addiction included:

• Genetic predisposition

• Other brain features that may make someone more vulnerable to addictive substances than the average person

• Psychological factors (e.g., stress, personality characteristics such as high impulsiveness or desire for pleasure, depression, anxiety, eating disorders, temperament, and other psychological factors). More and more risk factors present, the higher a person's chance of contracting the disease.

Although psychological and environmental factors seem more important in deciding whether a person is starting to use drugs, genetic factors seem to have more impact in determining who is going from drug use to addiction.

CAN ANYONE GET ADDICT AGAIN?

Many experts think 'Yes' is the answer. Many drugs are so highly addictive (e.g., nicotine, heroin), that prolonged or frequent use of them can cause addiction to anyone. Many people who try drugs or alcohol are not progressing to heavy use or addiction, though.

But by' climate,' what exactly does one mean? By definition, the environment refers to the circumstances or conditions surrounding an individual. It is a rather vague, blanket term which is often used to indicate the immediate surroundings of a person, generally consisting of a place containing people and things. However, researchers broke down the definition of "environment" into four primary domains: the domain of the family, the domain of peers, the domain of work or school, and the domain of community.

The peer domain is the social group of an individual and the places one gathers with peers. Friends and peers who misuse alcohol or drugs are the most significant contributor to the creation of a substance abuse problem.

So it should come as little surprise that peers could also prove to be such a destructive influence. Yet parents can be as instrumental in healing an alcoholic as they can be when coping with an alcohol or drug addiction. Specifically, it can be found that sober peers and friends who help treatment offer encouragement and inspiration to recover individuals. Similarly, recovering people are encouraged to pursue relationships with other recovering friends as this provides them with people they can connect to, give, and receive support in times of need or confusion.

The family role in a person's addiction is often reserved for biology or genetics discussions. But while we are genetically linked to our loved ones, there's no denying that the members of one's family also make up the overall home life or home environment. The domain of the family refers to the social and detailed features of a family rather than any genetic material which can be transmitted between them, and there is no doubt that the domain of the family can have a significant influence on whether or not an individual develops a problem of substance abuse.

While the peer domain is synonymous with the preferred social circle of an individual, the area of one's job or school refers to the conditions–and the occupants of the environment–to which he or she is attached. A person's approach to work or school will be different from what it would be at home or with friends, and relationships with employers or fellow students are generally far less intimate.

Meanwhile, as school environments appear to be more competitive and consist of highly concentrated populations, the school realm of teenagers and college students may become much more critical.

Society is the fourth and final domain, and another very significant potential cause of alcoholism and drug addiction exists too. The degree to which a person is addicted will contribute to the community domain is dependent on the extent of an individual's engagement with his or her society. Additionally, neighborhoods, where there is very little substance abuse, would have minimal risk of inducing substance abuse on an individual.

It's hard to identify one specific environmental factor that's to blame for addiction. In reality, people are likely to develop habits because of influences coming from all angles at them. But what's important is to be conscious of the many possible causes so one can take the necessary steps to minimize them, steering away from what is too often fatal disease.

1.4 Why pregnancy is a psychological war between mother and the baby

What better sight than a mother breastfeeding her baby? For passion, friendship, and boundless sharing, what better symbol could one find?

As a fetus grows, its mother consistently receives notifications. Not only does it hear her pulse, and whatever music she can play on her belly, it also receives chemical signals through the placenta. Researchers have found in recent decades that the setting in which a fetus develops in–the womb of the mother– is very significant. Many consequences are clear. For starters, smoking and drinking can be devastating. But others are more subtle; studies have found that people who were born during the 1944 Dutch famine, most of whom had starving mothers, were likely to have health issues such as obesity and diabetes eventually.

The emotional state of a pregnant woman— especially her stress, anxiety, and depression — can affect the development of her child, with long-lasting consequences.

Now, if we link this with the issue of addiction during pregnancy in mothers, we can develop the fact that addiction of any kind also has a profound impact on humans even before conception.

Addiction is a progressive, chronic disease with compulsive behavior, adverse side effects, and recurrence.

Like other illnesses, abuse poses severe risks to pregnant women and their children. Drug dependence is one of the most severe forms of addiction.

Co-occurring mental health disorders, which are commonly associated with alcohol, often pose unique challenges to health care. Eating disorders, depression, and other co-occurring disorders may cause physical changes that disrupt the prenatal child's development. Any material a woman absorbs may be passed to her baby while she is pregnant. Alcohol, tobacco, and other substances can go through the placenta— the baby's nutritional and oxygen-providing organ— and cause serious problems. Females who are pregnant, or who expect to get pregnant should, therefore, avoid drug drugs and inquire about a safe diet and lifestyle with their health care provider. Those who can't quit using alcohol or other medications will seek immediate care.

Addiction treatment during pregnancy can mean the difference between having a healthy child and losing a baby or giving birth to a child with severe developmental disabilities. While many pregnant women and teenagers are afraid of the repercussions of disclosing their drug or alcohol use, the fact remains that healing from substance abuse is far better than giving birth while being actively addicted. Alcohol and drugs can cause severe complications during pregnancy, as well as damage to the fetus ' physical and cognitive development. Furthermore, pregnant women and girls are exposed to violence, corruption, legal discrimination, and infectious disease through a continuum of substance use and addiction.

Vital nutrients and oxygen are transferred from mother to baby through the placenta, a layer of tissue, and blood vessels lining the uterus throughout the growth of a fetus. The placenta serves as a lifeline for the growing fetus along with the umbilical cord. The toxic compounds in alcohol, tobacco, cocaine, heroin, and other substances may also cross the placenta, impacting the infant. Additionally, these compounds can damage the placenta itself, interrupting nutrient exchange, and removing waste materials.

Babies born exposed to drugs or alcohol before birth become more vulnerable to developmental delays, learning problems, and behavioral disorders as they grow older. These may also have a higher risk of sudden infant death syndrome (SIDS) and other causes leading to premature death.

Studies show that drug use— legal or illegal— has a direct effect on the fetus during pregnancy. Whether you smoke, drink alcohol, or eat caffeine, the embryo will do likewise. If you're using marijuana or crystal meth, your fetus also feels the impact of these dangerous drugs— and if you're cocaine-addicted, you're not just putting your own life on the line, but you're risking your unborn baby's health. The effects of cocaine use include heart attacks, respiratory failure, strokes, and seizures. Such life-threatening health issues can be passed on to an unborn baby too.

In pregnancy, taking drugs often increases the likelihood of congenital disabilities, premature babies, underweight babies, and stillborn births. Early childhood exposure to marijuana and alcohol has been proven to cause behavioral problems. Such medications can also influence the memory and alertness of the infant. Moreover, some findings indicate that babies born to women who use cocaine, alcohol, or cigarettes while pregnant may have changes in brain development that continue into early adolescence.

Although the effects of cocaine are typically immediate, the impact that it can have on a fetus can last a lifetime. Babies born into mothers who smoke crack cocaine during pregnancy usually have their own set of physical and mental problems. The National Institute for Drug Abuse studies shows that there may be subtle, but essential, deficiencies in later children exposed to the drug in the womb. These deficiencies generally occur in areas such as cognitive performance, information processing, and task concentration. These are fields which are essential not only to the success of school but also to life.

Here are a few of the common consequences of drug use during pregnancy:

• Low birth weight puts a child at higher risk of disease, intellectual disability, and even death.

• Premature birth increases the risk of infant lung, hearing, and learning difficulties.

• Congenital disabilities often caused by drug use include hallucinations, strokes, and mental and cognitive impairments.

• Fetuses may become reliant on the drug(s) used by the mother and may experience symptoms of withdrawal after delivery;

Drug use can affect the developing organs and fetal limbs during early pregnancy. Just one episode of drug use during this time will affect your child's development. It refers in most cases to a congenital disability or miscarriage. Drug use can affect the progress of your baby's central nervous system later in pregnancy. Some medications can move through breast milk during birth and can harm the baby.

You want your baby as healthy as possible, as an expectant mother. Note, most of what you eat is transferred to your growing baby. Although some things are right for your baby, others might be harmful. For a developing baby, alcohol and illegal drugs are known to be particularly dangerous. Any volume of those substances during pregnancy is considered unsafe. When you are pregnant, you should stop them entirely. Quitting before you get pregnant is best, but your baby will benefit from avoiding drug or alcohol use at any stage during pregnancy.

Chapter 2: Trauma Bonding, Pathological Narcissism and self-isolation

For years, brain chemical dopamine has been called the "pleasure chemical" of the brain, sending signals between brain cells in such a way as to reward a person or animal for one action or another. More recently, research has shown that this effect is amplified by certain substances such as cocaine and heroin-an activity, which may lie at the heart of drug addiction.

Using advanced brain-scanning and a carefully controlled way to cause muscle pain, the researchers demonstrate that the dopamine system in the brain is highly active. At the same time, someone is experiencing pain-and that this reaction differs between individuals in a way that is directly related to how the pain makes them feel. It's the first time dopamine has been connected to human pain response.

If people are in distress, they often get lost.

Addiction is an isolated disorder. Solitude and isolation can cause addiction. Our own words sometimes get the sharpest tongues. It's hard to be inside our heads: a place where the cruel words and doubts are without limits. It is a place that is hard to escape–especially when it involves addiction.

Either it leads to self-isolation or in other situations it induces trauma bonding to be similar to Stockholm Syndrome, in which people held hostage come to have feelings of trust or even love for the very people who captured and held them against their will. In a partnership, this form of survival strategy may also occur. It is called trauma bonding and may happen when a person is in a narcissistic relationship.

In a trauma relationship, the spouse of the narcissist-who often has issues with codependency-first feels loved and cared for. But this starts to erode over time, and the link takes over from social, mental, and sometimes physical abuse.

Let's take a closer look individually at all these circumstances.

2.1 System of pain and pleasure- Addiction

What is the function and meaning of addictive pleasure?

For the past 5000 years, enjoyment has been associated with addiction. The explanation is that conventional forms of addiction are often pleasurable, such as drinking alcohol, taking other substances, playing games, and finding sex. Historically, this surface relation has led people to conclude that anyone who is genuinely motivated to drink, take drugs, and so on, must be looking for even more fun. It's a short step from there to conclude that addicts are unethical hedonists, individuals who pursue personal gratification regardless of the cost of even their existence to those around them. That is all wrong, of course.

Addiction is not about fun, though some of the very people who suffer from addiction believe it is.

But with this logic, the thinking of a moment shows the problem. Practically everybody likes alcohol influence. Most people love alcohol influence, yet are not alcoholics. Yes, would most of us be alcoholics if enjoying alcohol were the reason for alcoholism? Drinking can't be the drug excuse.

Addiction is, in essence, nothing more or less than a very healthy way of trying to deal with the overwhelming feelings of powerlessness. If coping mechanisms malfunction, we call them signs, like addiction, does. Addiction, like other signs we all have, is neither more nor less than a psychological symptom, a way of dealing with a problematic emotional condition. It doesn't have anything to do with getting high, being gratified, or having any other kind of fun.

Pleasure centers within the brain range from deep brain systems below the consciousness level to the brain's highest functioning thought areas. We include the Default Mode Network, a resting state of mind, where we have a real sense of who we are. The pursuit of pleasure is a fundamental imperative to live. This invests in well-being and meaning and is the primary motivation for social connections. Psychological principles involved in pleasurable action are to like and desire. Pleasure and satisfaction come from finding the balance between love and want. If desiring becomes the joy of driving force is lost. It starts as a pleasurable activity becomes an absolute requirement to obtain the experience. It's a need that's so high it's overwhelming because nothing else matters but having the object of desire. It causes unhappiness and is the driving force behind addictive disorders.

Happiness strikes a balance between relaxing and calming. We need to prioritize our needs and consider what matters most for us. The development of self-relieving techniques is of great importance for those who have lost this balance. While some addictions require abstinence as a strategy (abuse of substances), it's not always practical (abuse of food). Recognizing that having something too much threatens satisfaction is a tactic in all situations. How do we establish an equilibrium for the desired object? Could balance become the desired object? Could enjoyment become the desired object? Was health the object of desire? Could well become the desired object? Can a happy tonsil become the object of desire? Hopefully, the secret to maintaining the balance between like and needing is to find value in not being addicted.

Drug and alcohol use often starts in the teen years. As a result, alcohol and drug users ' brains are "hyper-stimulated" at an early age, and that level of "pleasure" becomes the norm over time. Teens are particularly vulnerable to this result, as the teen's brain is not yet fully developed. The teen's limbic system— the part of the brain that is emotional, reward / pleasure-driven is very adult-like. Yet, until the early to mid-twenties, the Prefrontal Cortex, the brain's "logical structure" where thinking, consequences, and future planning reside, is not entirely maturing. When the Limbic System becomes hyper-stimulated continuously by the use of drugs and alcohol, this becomes overwhelming and overrides the reasoning centers of the brain. Nonetheless, research shows that the use of drugs and alcohol slows the Prefrontal Cortex's maturation and growth.

Why do those dealing with substance abuse and their loved ones get this vital information? Because it helps explain why so many stupid, illogical, self-centered, and self-destructive activities include addicts. The Limbic System is dominant, with the logic system taking a back seat. It's "limbic vs. rationality," pleasure-seeking vs. rational thought, and the Limbic System wins a lot of the time in the addicted brain. It doesn't care about consequences or future goals— it just looks for the next rush of pleasure. And the Limbic System doesn't like getting any joy after years of hyper-stimulation. It has become so used and tuned to the rush of alcohol and drug use that it becomes dull and inevitably stressful, or even unbearable, in contrast, regular life. That's why many addicts come to the point where they say, "I feel miserable when I don't drink or use." The challenge is that addiction radically changes the chemistry and wiring of the brain. With the mind they have now, an addict can't recover — we need to help them rewire and readjust their brain back to normal levels of satisfaction where regular everyday life is fun and fulfilled.

Drugs and alcohol are highly potent neurobiological agents. We believe that we have found a magic bullet the first time we use — a way to hack the most fundamental force of all living beings as we push towards happiness and away from the suffering. A love affair starts when the influx of pleasurable neurochemicals fills our systems.

When this artificial force wears down our natural neurotransmitter supply, we're left feeling less than the whole. We want more euphoria, and that is what we want now. Cravings plague the prefrontal cortices. Rationality has gone out of the window. We need to end the pain. And so we continue our descent into the addictive pit.

Yet all emotions are fleeting, from transcendental ecstasy to existential despair. By their very definition, states of consciousness come and go. Hunting for fun, beauty, and joy is ordinary. In recovery, we need to learn how to build enjoyment, elegance, and happiness in real and tangible ways to add profundity and intent to our lives.

2.2 How do self-isolation destroy us?

Both humans are social beings, whether you call yourself a social butterfly or a wallflower. There is hardly a moment in your life when you don't communicate with another person or profit from their activities. Therefore, it is no wonder that our happiness coincides with our friendship with others.

Many people are at an all-time high of feelings of loneliness and turn to drugs or alcohol to self-medicate and numb painful emotions. Addiction, however, is an incredibly lonely disease that only leads to more excellent isolation.

Our own words sometimes get the sharpest tongues. It's hard to be inside our heads: a place where the cruel words and questions are without limits. It is a place that is hard to escape–especially when it involves addiction.

Isolation and loneliness impact drug addiction and alcoholism greatly. Research has shown that those of us who feel more socially isolated usually struggle with elevated problems of mental health and substance abuse. The reverse also holds: drug and alcohol addiction maybe not only an isolation effect but also a source of isolation.

Most people turn to drugs because they're lonely-and many people are depressed because they're drug-addicted.

For active addictions, isolation is widespread. People can turn to drugs because they are lonely and have other related difficulties. As the addiction disease progresses, the abuser may have a challenging time communicating with other people, resulting in more excellent isolation and loneliness. The desire to use alcohol or other substances is so intense that the user slowly becomes more and more disconnected from anybody or anything that gets in the way. None can compete at all costs with the urge to get high or to escape from reality. The further you go down into addiction, the less of a bond you have to other people. You want to be left alone when you want to do what you want, and you want to avoid confrontation with others. You should avoid hearing other people tell you that you are doing something wrong when you're alone. We cannot object to it so long as they can't see what you're doing. Isolation, therefore, becomes like a curtain around you that no-one can get through. If possible, you cut yourself off from other human beings. It's an incredibly lonely place to be.

Addiction and solitary confinement go hand in hand. Addicts want to have their addiction there. Nor must it be in a dusty barn or hidden in a dark basement. The alcoholic can be secluded in a crowded room or at a party. There is a detachment to addiction, a hands-off nature that distinguishes the addict from the rest of the world.

Many people see isolation as a psychological discomfort that is induced by a perceived lack of intimate relations. It's a real motivational force, similar in many ways to your physical need for food or sleep. That's why rejection experiences can cause the same part of your brain that is associated with physical pain. When you believe the need for belonging is not fulfilled, then isolation is a normal reaction.

We're telling ourselves to lie after lie despite our addictions. We are persuaded that we are too much or too little; that we must, we deserve, go through the fight of an upward struggle all by ourselves.

"I'm too much to deal with"... Lying.

"I'm a burden"... Lying.

"No one needs to resolve my struggle"... Lying.

"I've got to go through this on my own"... Lie.

The need to hide, with no escape in sight, leaves us trapped amid our addiction. The trouble with isolating ourselves during active addiction is that we keep reinforcing the lies the drug tells us. The medicine tells us that we need this, that without it, we cannot survive. We have to lock everyone and everything else out of our hearts and minds to keep that outlet in our lives. It's crazy what tricks addiction can play on us, like a master manipulator removing us from any lifeline around. The enemy is whatever comes in between our addiction.

Isolation can feel a lot like being in fasts, and: the more we combat it, the more we sink. Our minds are asking us to give in; our addiction is urging us to live alone.

Isolation is one of the main anti-recovery antagonists. Recovery asks us to move into the sun, welcome others on the sobriety path, admit our impotence, and acknowledge vulnerability.

Isolation assures us that we don't have to do any of those things so that we can stay perfectly content in our pain's hidden hiding place forever. The very first move to surmounting addiction is to conceal and accept the help and love not only from others but from ourselves.

There's a maxim in rehab rooms that says, "Addiction is the only illness that shows you you're right." One of the addicts ' coping habits is their tendency to withdraw. Most of the people involved in treatment understand the role of meetings, support groups, counseling, and religious services in combating one aspect of self-related addiction.

Addiction affects every aspect of one's life— work duties, responsibilities at home, parenting, romantic relationships, family issues, health, finances— it's all impacted. All too often, we see someone we love or a friend with an illness, and maybe they do not discuss personal problems as much as they used to. They may keep to themselves and may look sad overall with their lives. We wish we could do something to help them, but they continue to maintain a negative cycle of isolation and loneliness. Another concern we may be asking ourselves is: why are they doing this? The solution could be simpler than you think when it comes to addiction.

Addiction has a social element to it, and if someone already feels nobody cares about it or that no one can do anything to support them, then addiction perpetuates itself. Therefore, in the future, isolation can be a precursor to addiction just as it can be a part of addiction that continues to replenish itself with drugs or substances. Separation can be both a prior and a priori. Isolation and social connections subject are justified as many people use addiction to deal with the unwelcome feelings of loneliness, lack of love, feelings of indignity, and more.

Isolation is one of the more commonalities in severe substance use disorders. Many people may feel shame in their use and isolate themselves further and further from friends and family to conceal their substance abuse and the consequences of being intoxicated. Others may find themselves pushing away people who know about their addiction because they are causing the drug itself to be used further. Others might have always preferred to be less social, with drug use in isolation as natural as watching a film alone on a Friday night without an incident.

It can often be a combination of all those circumstances and more. Every one substance abuse case is precisely like any other case, just as one cold case is exactly like another. Most addiction-related habits may also include specific causes, right down to the normal behavior of an individual before drug use disorders develop. For some people, trauma may result in' self-medication' manifesting in disease because the injury has never been addressed. Others may experience trauma after they realize that they're addicted to some substance, like cocaine.

It can be internalized to isolate oneself when using it. Holding a secret from even your closest family members can emotionally separate a person from someone they respect and trust, also if the relationship itself continues with communication and even laughter daily.

The truths of loneliness and depression in addiction will leave those feelings to people:

• Feeling unable to communicate with anyone–physically or emotionally

• Feeling isolated from others

• Feeling sad that nobody can talk, be with you or understand

• Feeling that nobody cares

• Feeling rejected

- Feeling as if nobody wants to be with you

- Feeling alone

- We are living in fear, denial, and guilt.

Trapped in those overwhelming emotions, you can see why violent, physically, and emotionally abusive actions and false bravado sometimes cover up their fears by people who are addicted to drugs and alcohol.

You've noticed that sentence, "Hurt people, hurt people." It affects those who struggle with addiction–and in effect, it damages those around them.

As the addiction disease progresses, many people lose friends and destroy family members ' relationships, leaving them vulnerable-physically, psychologically, and even spiritually.

2.3 Addiction to Trauma Bonding

Have you ever remained in a relationship you know that if the tables were turned, you would demand that your partner get out?

In the beginning, it's exhilarating. When a surge of new feelings for someone new comes on fast and furious, the anticipation can be all-consuming. However, when that chemical wave begins to feel more like a destructive tsunami, understanding how to get back to dry land is critical.

This sequence of events can occur so rapidly that a person avoids even being swept up in the storm of a narcissist. What is it that makes these dangerous individuals just so magnetic? And why is breaking a bond with this type of person so hard?

If you have ever experienced a relationship that made you doubt whether it was love or violence, then you have encountered a trauma bond's toxic strength. This particular method of coercion is characterized by repetitive behaviors, in which the narcissist operates in a destructive cycle, which results in a trauma connection strengthened with every recurrent misdeed.

If you are involved in an abusive relationship, a painful bond develops, and the abuser becomes an integral part of your life. There are widespread abusive relationships, and the figures are troubling.

More positively, many people struggled to abandon their partners in those relationships for a variety of reasons. Maybe they were afraid their partner would do them harm. They may have lived because they had kids. But the desire for love and the cyclical promises of acceptance and affection are among the main reasons for staying in an abusive relationship.

Abuse occurs on a loop. Living with an abuser (or sharing space with him) isn't always evil, but still healthy. If you had been poorly treated throughout a relationship, you probably wouldn't stay. There are so many abusive partners where the abuser often threatens the victim with kindness (usually following an abusive incident). In the link, the abused continue to obey their abuser's "rules" until the next "heart" moment. But the truth is that violence is not love in itself.

Traumatic bonding is a condition where the survivor remains close to their attacker based on attachment and hormones triggered amid the abuse. During the relationship's traumatic stages, the survivor has elevated levels of cortisol. The victim feels like they're on the brink, believing their attacker can hurt or leave them if they don't listen. They look desperately for the reward hormone dopamine, which is a chemical for pleasure. When the abuser extends love to the victim, they are rewarded with dopamine, which further reinforces the traumatic bond. How are you breaking the cycle? The survivor should receive assistance in the form of therapy or individual counseling to start taking steps to end the relationship and start healing. You need not go through this alone.

A trauma bond is a bond that develops typically with a toxic person due to intense, emotional experiences. Similar to the Stockholm Syndrome, it holds us emotionally prisoner to a manipulator who keeps us "hostage"–whether through physical or psychological violence. Trauma bonds are common in dysfunctional, abusive, or otherwise toxic relationships. We are generally compounded by occasional encouragement, frequent love-bombing, false promises, or "small kindnesses" that a manipulator throws our way into the relationship to keep us engrossed. They, too, maybe compounded by our wounds of abandonment.

Among the most stubborn aspects of life is the creation of healthy connections and relationships with others. Things can get even more complicated when combined with a traumatic past. A person who has experienced trauma also develops an unhealthy allegiance to others, which is called the bonding of shocks.

Bonding with abuse can be a severe problem to deal with in therapy because it can become an unrecognizable addiction.

It is not surprising then that many individuals who undergo trauma bonding are fraught with tension, confusion, or abuse from early childhoods. If people repeat a pattern that they encountered first at the hands of violent parents with a romantic loved one, they can be said to retraumatize themselves. The biological model suggests that repetitive stressful events affect our neurochemistry and may cause us to replay stressful circumstances as a means to preserve emotional homeostasis (i.e., we become familiar with high stress and conflict and become "comfortable").

You know the cycle: things are bad and never seem to be getting better. The fights get worse, the insults get stronger and more personal, and the abuse becomes more pronounced. You feel helpless and weak, but you can't go.

Why is this all so hard when it seems so straightforward for everyone else?

While many of these relationships are blamed for trauma bonding or the secure emotional attachment that exists between an abused person and their abuser, the reality may be that addiction to love is to blame.

And what does the difference between the two means, and how do you know which one is that applies?

If people think of unconditional love, they tend to imagine positive images of mom or life-long friends who are caring. The relationships have a strong bond in these circumstances, based on values such as confidence, commitment, and, more than anything: mutual love.

But not all unconditional love created by bonding is safe-this unconditional love is harmful and toxic when a narcissist is involved.

Why are people staying with narcissists in abusive relationships?

How are you just not allowed to leave?

A significant part of the answer lies in the bonding of trauma: creating an unconditional love that you don't share with anyone else on earth.

This is the chain that prevents you from going "No Contact." It's not your fault, and with you, there's nothing wrong, but you can take control of the situation.

You may be in a trauma relationship with a toxic person; here are five signs:

1. You know they're tricky and conniving, but you can't seem to be letting go.

4. You try anything you can to satisfy them and are loyal to a fault even if they give you nothing but pain in return.

3. You find yourself addicted to them, and you lose far more than you gain.

4. They drive you to the brink of self-destruction.

5. You forget your worth and value–and you are willing, time and again, to lower your standards for this toxic person.

2.4 Pathological narcissism and addiction: A self-psychology perspective

Narcissism is a characteristic of character that determines the perception and interpretation of others of a person's self. Such as the small lens in a microscope, it is causing a person to focus in a very self-centered manner on the universe. They lose sight of notions like us, us, and compassion for others. It is a trait that takes hold early in the life of a person-typically as a result of a primary caregiver's significant breach of trust. Through this breach of faith, the individual vows never again to be vulnerable and set out to be an autonomous, self-supporting entity.

Even if narcissism is resistant to change, it may "soften" to the point where it no longer harms the quality of the person's life and relationships through a variety of clinical interventions. The individual can then accept a holistic plan of life rehabilitation through this softening, rather than feeling disconnected and removed from the healing power of others.

In searching for pathological narcissism, clinicians are searching for people who demonstrate the following characteristics:

• They are what they possess: they define themselves or themselves from the outside in. Through objects, public acceptance, and adoration from others, they find their self-worth.

• They are emotionally volatile: Only when they are appreciated and remembered as unique is the person happy. If challenged, they cannot handle being criticized and respond with anger.

• They are guided externally: There is no moral or intuitive compass for the individual. Rather than moral values, they are motivated by economic conceptions of performance.

• They are emotionally shut off: Empathy and compassion are missing for the individual. We think about others when we believe their attention is going to advance their selfish agenda.

• They are manipulative: the individual can be very charming and charismatic, but only for the sake of controlling and exploiting others.

• They're grandiose: they feel unique and special to the user. A condescending and dismissive attitude toward others is a tool they are using to build up themselves.

• They are entitled: The person feels they deserve special treatment and bonuses without paying or receiving duties.

• Constant attention is needed: The individual is continually seeking external validation and wants to be the focus of attention.

The more we know about narcissistic personality traits, the more we can understand the psychological reasons which cause people to stay in unhealthy ties.

The process of a narcissist is an addictive pattern, fostering a need for affirmation while leading their spouse to believe that toxic behaviors are usual. This cycle can be outlined in three phases: the partner's infatuation, devaluation, and rapid discard. The period becomes poisonous as the partner starts to crave the love that marked the start of the relationship, propelling them to forgive quickly and doing anything to get the partnership back to a place of good feelings.

A narcissist leverages inconsistent positive reinforcement to lure their partner back, as the pattern repeats. This cycle often becomes a relentless pursuit of winning back the first love and admiration that once abounded. By the time rationality sets in, and it's clear that the relationship has to end, victims still feel too helpless to escape.

Fast everyone on the planet has a bit of self-love, at least. That's the aspect that gives people trust and magnetism, and it's the kind of trait of personality that can make a person look attractive or even healthy. Yet modesty is also an essential part of a healthy adult's character, as it allows people to respect others and balance the self's needs against the needs of the whole community. When that balance is disrupted, and people love themselves more than their friends, there could be narcissism at play, and that could lead to addiction.

There is no single drug that tends to lean more on people with narcissism than any other. Alternatively, people like this tend to take in the same types of substances that are common among all drug users, including

- Alcohol

- Cannabis

- Cocaine

- Prescription drugs

- Methamphetamine

- Heroin

People with narcissistic personality disorder (NPD) automatically see themselves as superior to others. They adopt an attitude of extreme self-confidence, marked by boastfulness, pride, and a fixation on themselves and their interests.

But a paradox lies at the very heart of the NPD. Whereas individuals with NPD tend to exude self-assurance, their egomania pretentions and flights are, in reality, a mask for deep-seated insecurity and lack of self-esteem. Under all of this, narcissists are the exact opposite of what they pretend to be.

Those with narcissistic personality disorder go through life guided by a particular agenda more than most human beings. To validate their conviction that they are unique, they need constant praise, attention, and appreciation. We urgently need that affirmation and are highly sensitive, real or imagined, to rejection.

Depressingly, many NPD patients turn to alcohol and drugs to alleviate their feelings of hopelessness, frustration, and anxiety. Drug and alcohol addiction is widespread among NPD sufferers, who are often too proud to admit that they have let their drinking or drug use get out of control.

Narcissistic personality disorder telltale signs include:

• Over-inflated ego, distorted sense of self-importance

• Boastfulness, a persistent need to talk about real or imagined successes

• An overwhelming demand for flattery and publicity

• A clear understanding of entitlement but not focused on accomplishments • Frequent feelings of jealousy towards others admired or successful

• High-sensitivity

Anyone using alcohol and drugs to cope with mental health problems can easily slip into dependency over time, and, if they don't get help, they are likely to do so. Addiction is a disease seeded by seeds of deep personal dissatisfaction and disillusionment, and NPD sufferers usually experience large amounts of such sentiments.

It is not comfortable being in a narcissistic relationship. You are supposed to be making them the focus of your life and give them the significant attention they need while overlooking your needs – unless doing anything for you is in their best interest.

Grandiose delusions allow the narcissist to escape deeper feelings of indignity and self-doubt. Because breaking the fantasy bubble will mean acknowledging these painful underlying feelings and fears, narcissists become excessively defensive and angry whenever somebody tries to give them a reality check.

As a result, people in the life of the narcissist learn to tread carefully by

• Ignoring remarks that are false or outright lies

• Going along with their delusions

• Stroking their ego with compliments and encouragement

The dream must be sustained. Still, because it is not valid, it requires constant effort to keep it going –the narcissist as well as the people in his or her life.

Narcissists surround themselves with people who will provide the constant, over-the-top praise necessary to confirm their superior status continuously. They also prefer people's companies which they can manipulate and control, both physically and emotionally.

We also exploit and harass others without any sense of shame or fault since we lack empathy for others. A belief in being superior gives them the freedom in mind to handle others. However, they like it.

You can only see the world from one viewpoint, and all the conditions of life: their own. So if from their point of view something is good or bad, they believe that opinion always holds for everyone else. If there is a difference in pictures, they feel their advice is right, and the idea of the other person is incorrect.

As you can imagine, it is also difficult for people with NPD to conform to society as their view of the world is so different from that of all the others. It can be challenging to maintain relationships and jobs because other people get fed up with their pride, deceit, unrealistic mentality, and lack of empathy.

That can cause a person with NPD to feel like an outcast when the star of the show is what they desperately want. This, in effect, may lead to abuse of drugs and alcohol in trying to cope with the contradictions between their fantasy and reality. Mental health issues and substance abuse commonly go hand in hand.

If a loved one is showing signs of NPD, a mental health professional must pursue a diagnosis. It is particularly critical if the individual also has a problem with substance abuse.

Because one of the NPD's hallmarks is that the person denies that they have a problem, the typical drug and alcohol addiction treatment approaches may not be as practical as it requires a person first to admit that they are addicted and need to change.

In this type of situation, treating the personality disorder as well as the addiction is necessary. You'll want to see your loved one being handled by dual diagnosis personality disorders specialists.

Chapter 3: Pathway of Addiction

Addiction is a compulsive behavior toward a drug or activity that causes gratification and pleasure. Confining addiction to drugs and alcohol is simple, but people often participate compulsively in expressions such as sex, video gaming, shopping, and so on. Addiction, like any other disease or illness, is treated as a medical condition–not a problem –and calls for treatment.

Substance or behavior addicts often give their addiction more attention than any other obligation. Abandonment can be relatively difficult for drug and alcohol users, as they will experience symptoms of withdrawal that may force them to retake the substance.

Quitting is also tricky for people engaging in addictive behaviors. For example, they become uncomfortable when refraining and display an irresistible urge to go back to them.

It's important to understand that you've become addicted to action or drug, so you can get treatment before your addiction causes serious harm to your health and life. Anyone can feel as if they are being bound to a particular substance, action, or actions. Luckily the good news is that medication for all sorts of addictions is available.

3.1 What are the most common addictions?

When we are talking about addiction, we tend to think of tobacco, alcohol, and drug addiction. Although many of us often make this connection, there are many other drugs and behaviors (or processes) to which people are addicted. Numerous people around the world, for example, are hooked on gambling, food, and even jobs.

According to drug experts and psychologists, let's look at the most common addictions that affect people today.

Addiction to tobacco: Tobacco contains nicotine, the most addictive component used in cigarettes. This form of dependency has the highest number of addicts. Because cigarettes are legal and have mild side effects, cigarettes are often believed to be less dangerous than other types of addiction. Tobacco is causing more deaths than other habits. While people who smoke know that smoking is harmful to their health, they still find it very difficult to resolve the temptation to stop, which is a clear indication of a problem with addiction.

Alcohol addiction Due to the way our society accepts social drinking, alcohol addiction can be challenging to determine. Although alcohol is legal, it can expose users to numerous health risks from potential abuse and addiction. The World Health Organization says alcohol leads to at least 60 types of diseases and accidents, including liver disease, collisions, crime, etc. Due to cheap costs and easy availability, alcohol consumption continues to increase. Too much alcohol can also cause an overdose that can ultimately lead to death.

Cannabis addiction Marijuana, or cannabis, is the illegal substance most widely cultivated, used, and trafficked. It has begun to become more socially acceptable since it has been legalized in several U.S. states. This should not, however, distract from the fact that it is a substance that is potentially addictive. The increase in marijuana dependence in recent years may also be due to an increase in potency. Marijuana can affect physical performance and cognitive development, permanently damage memory, worsen schizophrenia, and cause a range of other problems.

Painkillers abuse several medications that are often administered to help alleviate pain by pharmacists and physicians, but the fact that they are prescribed does not mean that they are free from addictive properties. Although an individual may take seemingly harmless levels of painkillers, this may eventually lead to addiction. Many people taking painkillers don't realize they're addicted until they try to stop taking them. This can turn into a difficult habit to treat once they are addicted.

Cocaine addiction Cocaine is a typical upper-class drug because it is typically very costly. Even if cocaine addicts are numbered in the United States is beginning to drop, this is occurring at a steady pace. This medication can cause a variety of health problems and is particularly harmful to the heart. Crack cocaine is a free cocaine base type usually blended with baking soda or other cheap substances. All heroin and crack cocaine ruined the lives of many.

Heroin addiction Heroin is often considered to be the worst drug a person could be exposed to. After all, a single dose of heroin can result in a person becoming addicted. People often think they can try it once or twice and stop it, but they don't understand how addictive and harmful it is. Heroin withdrawal can be a terrible experience, which is why breaking the habit can be even harder for people. Heroin can cause many health problems such as kidney or liver failure, heart valve bacterial infections and blood vessels, and problems with the lungs. The sharing of needles can also lead to HIV, hepatitis B, and C.

Gambling addiction is a form of behavioral addiction involving various types of gambling that compromise the life, family, and career of a person. Gambling addicts tend to hide their behavior, which may include lying to members of their family or hiding losses or winnings. They use gambling to get arousal and excitement or as an escape. The addicts to gambling can face financial, legal, career, and interpersonal problems. Also, many people with a gambling problem may think about suicide or even attempt it.

Sex addiction can occur in a variety of ways, including anonymous sex with multiple partners, compulsive masturbation, prostitute sex, voyeurism, and affairs. This happens when a person is obsessed with sex and acts on their sexual impulses, without taking into account the damaging consequences. Sex addicts like to use sex to relieve their fear, escape reality, or fulfill compulsions that might be associated with a borderline personality disorder. Sexual addiction can lead to an increased possibility of contracting sexually transmitted infections and a tendency to engage in high-risk sexual behaviors.

Internet addiction is transforming Internet addiction into a global problem. Many people use the internet daily, but when it turns into obsession, it becomes a point. Internet addicts spend too much time online and ultimately give priority to their mates, families, careers, studies, and other activities with Internet usage. When it comes to their Internet habits, they begin to feel out of control and end up feeling guilty or behaving secretly. We may even experience symptoms of withdrawal, such as frustration or anxiety unless they use the internet for some time.

Binge Eating Disorder: Food Addiction For years, it is argued that food obsessions may be food addictions— or that this "disorder" is more of an excuse. Binge eating disorder is indeed a real problem affecting adults. Symptoms include eating emotions to ease, overdoing food while alone, and feeling guilty after the binge. The cause of eating disorders is unclear, but it possibly relates more to depression than to addiction.

Risky Behavior Addiction Thrill seekers share many of the same symptoms as drug addicts; they get a rush from skydiving or climbing rock, but after a while, they are looking for even more dangerous adventures to feel the same level of excitement. And studies show that those thrills fill the brain with the same chemicals that addictive drugs produce.

Video Games

A video game addict plays video games to the point that this practice influences his or her life. The most addictive video games are those where players assume a character's identity in the game and can communicate with other players.

3.2 Heredity, Environment, & Susceptibility to Addiction

Addictions are a highly complex set of common diseases bound together to some degree by mutual etiological factors in genetics and the climate. They're also recurrent, with a pattern of relapsing/remitting. Genetic studies and other analyses that clarify the roots of addiction help destigmatize addiction, resulting in more prompt treatment. Knowledge of genetic factors in etiology and response to treatment may allow prevention and treatment to be individualized, as well as new therapeutic targets to be identified.

Why are some people getting addicted while others are not? Family studies involving identical twins, fraternal twins, adoptees, and siblings show that as much as half the risk of becoming addicted to nicotine, alcohol, or other drugs depends on the genetic makeup of the person. Finding the biological basis for this vulnerability is an essential avenue for researchers trying to resolve the drug addiction issue.

At least half the susceptibility of a person to drug addiction may be related to genetic factors.

When researchers seek "addiction genes," they look for biological differences that can make a person more or less vulnerable to addiction.

Everyone responds differently to drugs and medicines. You've probably already seen it. Say you are taking a prescription, and it works fine. But for one mate, the same medication does nothing, making another feel sick. Gene variations often cause variations such as those.

As scientists look for genes linked to addiction, they check genetic variations associated with these forms of responses. A vulnerable person might have a strong preference for a given drug. Or if they try to quit, they experience extreme withdrawal symptoms. On the other hand, when a person feels no gratification from a drug that makes others euphoric, he is less susceptible.

Disorder of alcohol use often exists within communities. That is because there is an inherited aspect, which means it can pass through genes from parent to child. For that reason, your family history offers hints as to how vulnerable you may be to addiction. For example, if you have an affected close relative, it is an indication that you need to be extra careful.

Scientists will never discover even one genetic modification that induces addiction. Substance use disorder, like most other disorders, is a complicated character. It is affected by multiple gene variations, plus the environmental factors.

Each person inherits a unique combination of variations of the genes. Individuals with substance use disorder may have different genetic underlying causes. So people who share specific variants of the high-risk genes may have the traitor may not.

Although identifying the exact genetic cause is elusive, multiple research lines do indicate that genes affect drug use.

It is essential to understand the full context of all potential risk factors when evaluating whether someone is vulnerable to substance abuse because a blood relative suffers from it.

Biological:

• Gene and environmental stressors on gene expression account for 40-to-60% of an individual's addiction risk, according to the NIH.

• There are five inherited mental illnesses: ADHD, autism depression, bipolar disorder, and schizophrenia. Undiagnosed or unmonitored mental illness is often a significant risk factor for drug abuse.

• The NIH estimates that while men are more likely to use illicit substances and have higher dependency levels, women may be at higher risk of addiction and relapsing.

• The medical community does not accept as a singular entity an "addictive personality."

• There are, however, a variety of personality traits that may coexist with addiction, including impulsive behavior, nonconformity, and behavioral, neurological, or psychological impairments.

Environmental:

• Early childhood experiences within the home and with the family significantly contribute to increasing the risk of substance abuse for an individual. Children exposed to harmful situations and abuse of drugs or alcohol by family members experience more behavioral problems, which often lead to experimentation.

• Peers and peers, especially teens, are powerful influencers. Even if a young person is not genetically predisposed, the desire to fit in, lack of proper supervision, inadequate social skills, and community poverty are vital contributors to his or her risk of substance abuse.

Just as biology isn't an actual cause of addiction, direct purposes aren't always a problem. Medical experts, for example, believe that most children who have parents with addiction challenges don't develop substance use disorders.

Trauma:

• Research indicates that children and adolescents with traumatic events are at higher risk for substance abuse.

• A shock reduces the ability to be resilient and cope with life challenges, particularly in a dysfunctional setting, unless adequately treated. It makes it more likely for a person getting self-medicated to deal with difficult circumstances or traumatic memories.

• Trauma is severe. This encompasses mental, physical or sexual abuse; neglect or negligence; domestic or social violence; sadness and other dramatic loss, and displacement by conflict, terrorism, or refugees.

• If someone is predisposed to substance abuse and suffers severe trauma, he or she may have trouble resisting the heavy use of drugs or alcohol.

The bottom line is this: no matter what genetic predisposition, there's not one-factor predicting addiction. It's usually caused by situations creating a domino effect that contributes to compulsive use. Once the disease changes the brain chemistry and function of an individual, any combination of behavior, social context, and physiology will need to be rectified for a full recovery.

Many individuals are not very familiar with their family history of addiction. The rest of the families are not concerned about abuse. You could have a rabid addict in your family not so long ago, and nobody would think about that. Or they'd make a harmless joke like, "Oh, he's drinking a little too much." Because there was so little people could do about alcohol, there was no point in talking about it.

But now that you can do something on addiction, it's worth talking about family history. Once you stop using it and tell your family, you're recovering, and it's often when they're going to tell you about the family secrets. That is when family members come out of the closet sometimes and tell you their tales.

Let your coping skills be your children's legacy. Don't let your genes be your children's only legacy. Because of your addiction, your children are more likely to have an addiction. But its genes need not be its destiny. By teaching them healthy coping skills, you can help your kids lead happy lives-by being an example of your recovery.

If you have a family history of dependence, you can become addicted to any drug. If at least one member of your family is addicted to alcohol, you are more likely to develop an addiction to any other medication, such as opioids, cocaine, or marijuana. Cross-addiction is caused by all habits working in the same part of the brain. If your mind is wired to predispose you to one addiction, you will be predisposed to all addictions.

This is especially significant for women who may come from alcoholic families but often develop addictions that go undetected, such as tranquilizer addictions, pain relievers, or eating disorders.

One addiction can lead to other habits, and one drug can cause you to relapse into another. That's one of the consequences of a wired brain on addiction. Suppose you are a cocaine addict. When you want to stop cocaine use, then all addictive substances, including alcohol and marijuana, will end. You may never have had any of them, but if you choose to use alcohol or marijuana, they may ultimately bring you back to your favorite drug. Recovery requires complete abstinence.

Individuals who associate with others who misuse drugs or alcohol are more likely to engage in this activity as well. And as the usage ebbs and flows in quantity and variety around an individual, so does their behavior. There are, however, many more environmental factors outside mates. Often ecological factors contributing to the addiction are parental influence, cultural norms, media representation, and acquired physical interactions.

If the social interactions of a person rely heavily on associating with individuals that show possible alcohol or drug issues, then it can be challenging to exorcize yourself by exhibiting equally troublesome behaviors. A significant factor in sustaining addiction is the sense of belonging and feeling associated with like-minded people.

3.3 Who am I? Addiction dims the existence of oneself

Addiction is pervasive and universal. That can hijack your whole life faster than you realize. This illness can infect every aspect of your existence in many ways.

Drug abuse has devastating effects on mind, behavior, and relationships. Still, the ongoing impact of drugs on the body can slowly destroy vital systems and functions, culminating in permanent disability, or even death. Even legal medicines, taken to excess, can cause significant problems that cannot be easily undone; and excessive consumption may not also be necessary for lifelong harm to occur for some illicit drugs.

Who are you, then? If you're drug-addicted, you mightn't know how to answer the question. Even if you're freshly sober, you might not be entirely sure. Drug treatment allows you to awaken intelligence, personality, faith, and more. But let's take a look at how drug addiction can make a person's identity lost.

The identity of a person is tricky. It's made up of how you see yourself, how others see you, what's there in spite of what you or others don't understand, and what no one can see. So, you generally don't know a good portion of your full identity as a human. There's nothing wrong with this; for everyone, it's just reality. Some people make the most of what they know about themselves and what they can accumulate from the perspectives of others.

When you bring in excessive quantities of drugs and alcohol, pieces of your identity start to get clouded. Second, the immediate effects of drugs and alcohol distort the memory of your acts and emotions in the short term. It adds to the aspect you don't know about yourself very clearly.

Your personal growth and maturity also form a part of your identity. That means challenging your ideas and beliefs, giving up some of them, and embracing new ones. Usually, this includes emotional pain, surprise, some distress, stress, and even confusion. Those interactions cloud drugs and alcohol and disturb the feelings. It reduces your ability to understand yourself and have self-esteem.

A person with drug dependence or alcoholism has tremendous loneliness in his or her life. That's more than likely why, first, they start drinking excessively. As a child or young adult, they might have felt the need to suppress some of their self-understanding and emotions. Sexual abuse, divorce, parents with mental illness, family chaos-any of these things may have disrupted their self-understanding process.

If depression gets too much, the suffering is covered up by drinking and drug use. It blocks an even greater understanding of oneself and personal growth. Their identity has long been fuzzy and disrupted; their use of drugs or alcohol becomes the most evident element of their character.

The addict loses all self-respect entirely. He (or she) no longer holds a high opinion of himself and no longer feels any respect for his goodness or worth, as in an addictive lifestyle, all honesty and value vanish. An addict manipulates and lies to others and himself, as the cravings drive him to do acts that he would never have dreamed of abusing substances before his life.

Addicts lose not only self-esteem but also the respect of those closest to them.

The reason is simple: Drugs and alcohol damage the brain. We fill the mind with dopamine, a neurotransmitter that is found in brain regions that control movement, emotion, motivation, and pleasure feelings. This causes the person who uses drugs or alcohol to feel moments of extreme happiness, but they are left with nothing but cravings once that feeling goes away. As the appetite for the drug continues to grow, to feel the euphoric effects, the person needs to drink more and more of it. It quickly turns into a vicious cycle in which the person uses continuously, yet never attaining their original high.

Drug and alcohol abuse alters vital brain activity over time and forces the brain to prefer the drug over everything else. Because drugs or alcohol consume the mind, the personality of an individual is drastically altered. Anyone who has a substance abuse problem often morphs into entirely different people.

Ways Drugs and Alcohol Can Affect Personality and Behavior Include:

• Secrecy

• Paranoia

• Restlessness

• Manipulation

- Forgetfulness

- Forgetfulness

- Shifting responsibility

- Becoming violent

- High-risk behavior

- Low-stress tolerance

- Frequent mood swings

Fatigue and negative personality changes can have devastating effects on an individual's behavior.

Addiction affects how we see ourselves, and in effect, takes away a degree of our understanding of ourselves. We cannot track and analyze our feelings, motives, and actions correctly anymore. For example, many people fighting addiction deny they have a substance abuse problem. Denial is a significant factor that contributes to a lack of self-awareness, which encourages the persistent use of drugs and alcohol, preventing successful rehabilitation.

3.4 Discovering oneself is the stepping stone in Recovery & Sobriety

Going physically healthy is the first step; next comes the mind and the emotions. If past events have caused you to feel ashamed, unworthy of love, lonely, or depressed, it's essential to search for self-discovery methods that will help you come to terms with your life choices and bring out positive parts of yourself that have been hidden or unknown for years.

Live an authentic life is when our actions and words adhere to our convictions and beliefs. It's being our true selves, not an imitation, not acting like we feel other people would accept or behave like others say we should. This works, performs, talks, and lives a life that is true to our identity. Opening oneself to authenticity means knowing one another and being frank about what we want from life. Whether we find ourselves living to win others ' approval, or compromise our ideals, principles, or convictions, we don't live an authentic life.

To sustain sobriety means maintaining a commitment to the well-being and personal and spiritual development. Live authentically is a practice that improves the overall sense of their lives and benefits people in recovery. It also ensures that we create an experience of which we can be proud, as we honor ourselves.

People recovering from addiction often lose self-esteem, which can lead to depression.

Women are likely to be deeply shamed by the effects of their alcohol or drug addiction, as they may have had children removed from their care. Or because of a host of other negative consequences, including DUI's, time in prison, job losses and relationships, and worked in the sex industry.

Their self-esteem and Sense of Self-awareness suffer during this time, and so do their families.

The path to a substance-free life is long for many addicted individuals and filled with difficult challenges. The rehabilitation of physical, emotional, and mental tolls can sometimes also make it feel like a futile effort. Mindfulness is critical, however, that a learning experience comes with each challenge, and a chance to grow. That's all part of self-discovery, as is the ability to tackle the impulses that led to drug or alcohol abuse and to learn the courage to stay away from triggers that could lead to a rebound.

Taking things gradually is one of the critical elements of healing. At first, trying to embrace a new, sober life and everything that comes with it can be so overwhelming; it's essential to pace yourself and remember that you're not your past. Let go of your mistakes and the decisions that led you down the path of substance abuse. Holding everything onto them would hinder your advancement.

To become self-conscious Self-consciousness is awareness of one's nature, thoughts, motivations, and desires. Knowing one's self is of the utmost importance in understanding what we value and how we can be honest with ourselves. Taking the time to be aware of our everyday habits and outline our passions can inspire self-awareness. Self-awareness links us with our highest self and inner realities that we can use as tools to live the best and most actualized possible life.

Just as a lack of self-awareness can prolong an addiction, self-awareness building can help in treating addiction when undergoing drug rehabilitation. Self-awareness enables you to understand both the root causes of your addiction and its triggers. As you become more conscious of these, you become better able to control your environment and thus gain control of your addiction.

To support your addiction treatment and promote full recovery, self-awareness can be strengthened and developed. The knowledge of your behaviors and patterns is an essential step toward developing self-awareness. In this case, individually, those trends that contribute to your use of the drug. Becoming more conscious of these trends helps you to alter them and avoid the use of drugs before they start.

A critical aspect of recuperating addiction involves working to restore self-awareness. It consists in trying to identify those patterns of behavior, negative thoughts, or false assumptions that precede substance use or alcohol use. Once these problems are identified, the patient may begin to develop coping mechanisms to improve his or her behavior; in other words, self-awareness helps prevent the recurrence of alcohol or drug use.

One common tactic advocated by counselors and therapists in treatment is what is known as the response to "Pause and Plan." As the name implies, when they spot one of their triggers, thoughts or behaviors that in the past drew them to booze or drugs, those who misuse substances are encouraged to "pause" If they can then "plan" their response, they can hopefully make decisions that are more in line with their priorities and expectations for recovery.

Through practicing mindfulness and knowledge of the present moment, we can be self-conscious. By journalizing about our goals, success, dreams, triggers, and desires, we can also become self-aware. The clearer we can be on living a life that alights with our reality, the more we become self-aware.

How to raise self-awareness. In several ways, people who are in recovery work on their self-awareness. Talking in one-on-one or group therapy sessions about their feelings and thoughts will help people gain insights into how to make meaningful changes in their lives. We may also keep a journal, practice the technique of "self-talk," or engage in art or music therapy to better put them in contact with what we feel and think.

If you want to make an effort to increase your self-confidence, here are five steps that you can take today:

1. Make time for self-reflection and introspection, which is the first step in understanding unwanted behavior.

2. Let your feelings be known–not just what they are, but what their root is. Beware of your answers or reactions to different situations.

4. Pay close attention to your thought processes, so you can start pausing and formulate appropriate responses rather than allowing your thoughts to dominate you.

5. Ask others for feedback, because they will probably notice something you don't have about you.

If someone you know denies their substance abuse, lectures and warnings will probably do no good. Only when their self-awareness starts to grow do they begin to recognize that for things to change, they have to make changes in their lives. When a person in recovery is self-conscious, he or she is far more likely to be motivated to embrace a treatment program, therapy regimen, and aftercare plan — and remain substance-free for good.

Mastering self-acceptance. Self-acceptance is feelings of self-satisfaction given shortcomings and whatever past habits and choices. Getting real about authentic living means uncovering and acknowledging wounds or errors with grace. It involves accepting our strengths and weaknesses as well as pointing them out as valuable parts of our being. They also don't equate ourselves to others because we see ourselves as individual beings that are still rising. Some have made mistakes and have suffered a lifetime of abuse, but understanding the recognition of past mistakes is essential to freedom of emotion.

There may be behaviors that you have that are unhealthy, but being mindful of your negative habits allows you to increase the quality of your life. Ask friends and family members for feedback on post-therapy progress, or for further guidance to find out who you are. While understanding how others see you, allowing yourself to be who you give feedback on whether you are authentic and genuine to your inner self.

Being Real To Yourself. Recovery is a time for looking very inward. This process does not end with a session of therapy; instead, it continues for the rest of your life every day. That might feel like a daunting task, but in reality, it's just a question of being honest with yourself and what you want.

Keeping a journal which no one else will see can be helpful. In it, write down your deepest fears, your highest dreams, the happiest and worst days that you can recall, and the things that you most want to achieve. Listing all the things you have already done can be beneficial too. Having them put out on paper will make them more appropriate, which can increase your self-esteem.

Ask yourself in the journal for non-judgmental questions, and answer them as honestly as possible. Remember, there's no one else going to read it.

Writing down any new areas you wish to learn about can also be helpful. Whether it is adopting a new language or becoming more spiritual, these opportunities to develop are crucial not to deny yourself. If you enjoy reading, consider spending time in a local library or bookstore and concentrate on a subject you would like more information about. Give yourself time to explore your abilities; perhaps you'll be shocked.

Recovery is a long road; a person in recovery would probably be there for their entire life. It won't always be straightforward, particularly if you don't feel within your family or friends that you have a support system, and there may be relapses of varying degrees. Remember to tell yourself that getting a decline isn't shameful and that it doesn't mean you're a loser. You are a mere human being. Everything that implies is you need to look inward to find the well of energy that first took you to recovery and start over again.

Chapter 4: Excessive Social Media Use Comparable to Drug Addiction

Social media started as a way for people to connect with friends and family, even though they were thousands of miles away. Nevertheless, it has changed over the years. Today, social media is being used in a variety of ways, and much more frequently. For example, it is used by corporations, non-profit organizations, and even politicians as a way of reaching a very focused audience.

Teenagers and young adults, meanwhile, use social media as a virtual scrapbook to record every detail of their lives as they live it. There are even large-scale social media "influencers" who use their followers as a way to promote a product, service, or community through social media and gain support for it. Social media is even a valuable resource to link isolated populations with other parts of the world and a connection to them.

Bad decision-making is a characteristic frequently associated with drug addicts and pathological gamblers, but what about individuals who use social media excessively?

Was overuse a probability to be described as a social media addiction? In terms of impairing decision-making, is this equivalent to drug addiction?

Impaired decision-making is often related to gambling or drug dependence. The new research suggests that heavy social media use is also correlated with poor decision-making skills.

Compared to drug addicts, heavy users of the social networking site (SNS) show concern with social media platforms when they don't use them, mood adjustment when they use these sites, and acceptance of the social benefits received from interactions on these sites. Such heavy SNS users often experience friction with others because of their use, and they exhibit withdrawal symptoms and often relapse while trying to leave. Perhaps notably, people with drug use and behavioral addictions are struggling to make value-based decisions.

Given these apparent similarities, the issue of whether inappropriate use of social media should be classified forever as an "addiction" is being hotly debated.

The idea of not being able to check their social media accounts causes some people to break out in a cold sweat. We become nervous and anxious and are unsure of how to handle the situation. Therapists also refer to this as a social media anxiety disorder when this happens, which may share similarities with a social anxiety disorder.

Among the most critical measures of social media, the issue is when it starts interfering negatively with your life. It is worth remembering that what you see on social media is just another person's highlight reel.

4.1 What this social network age is doing to our generation

Our world was never connected any more than it is today.

With even more than 4.4 billion Internet users across several types of devices, nearly two-thirds of the world's population is plugged into the matrix. We are using these tools for work and play — and social media have altered the way we communicate online and offline.

During the last decade, browsing and scrolling via social media have become an increasingly popular practice. While the use of social media by most people is non-problematic, there is a small percentage of users who become addicted to social networking sites and indulge in excessive or compulsive use Addictive social media use will look much like any other substance use disorder, including alteration of mood (i.e., social media interaction contributes to a favorable change in emotional states).

The term "addiction" makes one think about alcohol and drugs. Yet, a new type of addiction has emerged over the last 20 years: addiction to social media. It may not cause physical damage, such as that caused by tobacco and alcohol, but it does have the potential to cause long-term harm to our feelings, attitudes, and ties.

While the older generation–those born shortly after World War II in the baby boom period–had alcohol and drugs as their addiction, the younger generation— the so-called Millennials — have social media as theirs. Born between 1984 and 2005, the millennials embraced the digital age, utilizing technology to relax and interact with others. To them, social media is a big deal; it's a lifeline for the outside world.

While people of all ages use social media, it is more detrimental to younger users than it is to older people.

As many parents are probably already aware, their teenage children can be completely addicted to social media. And with the different websites and the variety of social media platforms, teenagers can sometimes spend the whole day glued to their phones. While I am not justifying the causes for teenagers to be trapped on social media all day, it is a worthy goal to enlighten others when attempting to raise awareness of the potential negative impacts of social media

The Fear of Missing out (FOMO), is possibly one of the first factors that come to mind when thinking about why our generation is addicted to social media. Although some do not care if they are the first to see a new post from someone famous in their community or even a celebrity, teenagers also pay a lot of attention to their phones so that they can see and understand what's going on in the pop culture world.

It's the fear that if many teens don't go on social media, they'll miss an important event or something they think is essential. Often in school, a student's peers may be thinking about a post or video they all saw and posted the day before, and if that student wasn't on social media at the time, they feel left out of the discussion, and not as involved in it as well.

One factor teenagers are concerned with social media today is because their accounts determine how they look to others. That is, the more people they like and follow, the more envious and famous they come off like others. Many teenagers may be actively searching for more followers on social media platforms, making their posts the best they can be, or finding a way to get more feedback on their posts.

One explanation teenagers might be addicted to social media is because they can connect with their peers quickly and easily, no matter where either of them is. With just a few buttons pressing, kids in my generation can send pictures to each other on Snapchat as well as gossip and speak via DMs (direct messages) or IMs (instant messaging). Teenagers can look as if they are addicted to social media, even if they don't because they spend a lot of their time talking online through these social media platforms with their peers.

Social media can serve as a real-world escape. If a teen is stressed, sad, or even depressed, they may turn to social media to forget about their problems, even if it's only a few hours away. It's also much easier to express yourself on social media, and teenagers who might be shy in real life are more likely to have a bolder online presence; they're able to think about their words and come off as witty, even if they're nothing like that in real life. Therefore, if a teenager feels lonely or distant from his or her family or friends, they can turn to social media.

It's easier to make friends on these sites, and more often than not, people are welcomed wholeheartedly and automatically, providing a kind of haven for those who feel this way. Most of the time, people post such events in their lives, whether positive, such as getting a job or going to college or sad, such as failing a test or having a loved one pass away, so their online friends and followers can comment and give them encouragement, support or reassurance.

A final reason adolescents will spend plenty of their time on social media, or on their phones in general, is to spend time avoiding boredom. Too many times at dinner parties or adult get-togethers do my sister, or I decide to spend the time on our phones and click through social media instead of just sitting there and doing nothing. I wasn't like we were trying to avoid people talking to it was merely the fact that no one wanted to speak to us. Instead of doing nothing in the hours these things took (and becoming utterly bored in the process), we make it upon ourselves to get sucked into our phones to give us something to do.

So, with all this in mind, it's painfully clear that a good portion of teenagers worldwide is addicted to their phones. Nevertheless, the implications of this are appallingly negative. The "good" people seen online tend to lower self-esteem among adolescents. We compare ourselves to others without even thought, especially the ones we see on social media platforms. If teens decide they're not "good enough" because they don't look a certain way, depression, anxiety, eating disorders, a hard time sleeping, disconnectivity, self-image fixation, drug use, isolation, and self-harm may manifest in teens.

Moreover, as teenagers spend a lot of their time on social media, they have fewer and fewer face-to-face experiences and relationships, and they experience all of that online.

While many people use social media regularly, very few are truly addicted. If you're worried that someone might run the risk of developing a social media addiction, ask yourself these six questions:

• Does he/she spend much time thinking about social media or planning to use social media?

• Does he/she feel encouraged to use social media continually?

• Is he/she using social media to think about personal issues?

• Does he/she still try, without success, to reduce social media usage?

• Incapable of using social media, will he / she become anxious or troubled?

• Will he/she use social media to such a degree that it has harmed his / her work or studies?

When you replied "yes" to more than three of these questions, then a social media addiction may or may evolve.

4.2 Do we depend on the attention we seek from social media to be happy?

Social media is a significant channel of communication in today's interconnected world and an essential part of daily life. There are so many positive aspects— not only does social media allow us to communicate quickly with loved ones and to catch up with friends, but it also provides entertainment, breaking news, and the latest topics from practically anywhere around the world.

At the same time, the way that social media networks are always trying to rate their users is a bit unsettling. How many people now have "liked" your post?

The desire to be socially accepted and admired can be too much to deal with and can adversely affect many social media users ' self-esteem. How do you feel when spending time scrolling through your Facebook, Instagram, or Twitter feeds? Enjoy social media, or are they a source of stress or frustration?

Of all the ways that social media can be corrupt for you, Facebook's potential, and the like to cause jealousy is one of the worst, according to science. You see your friends posting happy selfies at exotic destinations and humbling about their professional and personal successes, and you end up thinking they don't calculate their own lives.

Of course, intellectually, we all know that our real-life selves and our highly curated online selves differ enormously. However, it's still easy to fall into the trap of letting the perfect social media profiles of other people convince you that somehow you're falling short. People would flock to Facebook to see the latest news about their wedding, new baby arrival, or home purchase. Many users go to their newsfeeds to passively watch and compare, research indicates, much more often than sharing their news or updates.

It turns out that some of us prefer to look at specific types of people and compare them to others: the ones who make us feel better about ourselves. And that, in effect, will lead to greater happiness and satisfaction in life.

We're always in the rat race, trying to post the best videos, pictures, and status updates to get the most views, follows, or comments. Underneath the craze of social media, however, we are merely trying to brag and write out the best moments of our lives, even when we may live in misery. We live in a world where we always equate our lives to others and sometimes take no time to consider our causes, losses, obstacles, successes, and accomplishments because we are so busy trying to present ourselves in the best way possible. We don't need to unwind for a moment, take a deep breath, and withdraw from the world. People rarely share their daily struggles on their social media accounts, partly because society is pushing us to showcase the best parts of our lives and not our challenges.

Can social media turn into addiction? Will representation of your Internet life wrongly raise self-confidence?

Hunger for favorable feedback. Chances are that when you wake up in the morning, you'll check your Facebook newsfeed; it's become a daily routine for many. Research has shown the effects of constructive brain reinforcement from social media activity. Interestingly, when they received positive, positive feedback about themselves, participants in a well-known study showed greater activation within the nucleus of brain accumbens than when they saw positive feedback from someone else.

Let's face it; it is challenging to resist positive reinforcement and can lead people to become addicted to Facebook or other social media sites. Throughout social media, status updates and photographs frequently show an idealized version of the reality of that person.

Thirst for instant gratification. Influencing what people post on social media sites is the desire for instant gratification, and the belief that bigger and better will bring happiness. It takes less than a second for our brain to determine whether we want to click right or left on a dating profile, based on the appearance of the other person, or if we wish to like a Facebook friend's post based on an image. If we are not overwhelmed immediately with gratification, then we will move on to something more gratifying, hence why we "swipe left," "unfollow," or "unfriend." This can cause users to continually compare themselves to others and care less about their own lives, potentially leading to negative feelings like envy or low self-esteem.

It seems teens are most hardly affected. Research studies have shown that teenagers who have been using social media for more than two hours a day are displaying signs towards a mental health disorder such as depression or fear. Although there is no proof of a clear causality, the data shows a correlation between social networking and adolescent depression. This may return to the theory of instant gratification and low self-esteem or may be due to the upcoming issue of cyberbullying that often occurs on social media.

Self-esteem. We all have our fair share of insecurities, some of which we speak openly, and some of which we prefer to remain with ourselves.

The relentless barrage of beautifully filtered pictures appearing on Instagram is bound to knock out the self-esteem of many people, while obsessively checking your Twitter feed just before bed may lead to poor sleep quality.

Yet comparing yourself to others on social media by stalking their esthetically beautiful Instagram photos or staying up-to-date with their Facebook relationship status could do little to assuage your self-doubt feelings.

4.3 What is happiness?

What is Bliss??? Definitely. What do you do to get happy?? Do you feel satisfied???

Happiness, in our lives, is something we all desire.

There are different answers to this question like "I'd be happy when I buy a new car, a new house, a new store, traveling the world, being with friends or family, winning a lottery, getting married, having children, playing, partying with friends, etc." Most of these moments come into your life for a couple of minutes or days, and then they're gone. Those are momentary joy like buying a car, shop or house and they can't make you happy for a long time.

Individuals get into relationships or marriages because, in their partner, they seek happiness. Then one day, you have had an argument or battle, and you feel your joy is gone.

We all want to be in their business with our friends and family because we feel happy.

We're looking for happiness in traveling and enjoying in various cities, catching scenic beauty in our cameras.

But you don't think your happiness is linked to worldly things, locations or other people.

And the fact is that we look to the outside world for our joy. We don't even understand what true happiness means.

True happiness is contentment within you. True happiness is loving your own business and living with your body, mind, and soul in peace and harmony. True happiness is a persistent state of mind being in love with yourself.

You need neither other men, nor worldly things to be pleased.

"Happiness is the result of personal striving. You struggle for it, you search for it, you rely on it, and sometimes you even look for it to travel around the world. You have to indulge in the embodiments of your gifts without yielding. And once you've reached a state of happiness, you never have to become lazy in preserving it. You will make a mighty effort to keep swimming up into that joy forever to live flat on top of it. "— Elizabeth Gilbert, Feed, Pray,

Love. If we take a moment to look at those around us, we can see that the absolute desire to be content and to escape misery is the common denominator that unites us all.

Looking at today's world, we could easily forget that being happy is the primary purpose of our life-you could call it the heart of being human. We all share the same wish to seek happiness and avoid suffering, and the same right. Even a desire for happiness is to pursue a spiritual path or religious life. To get us delight, we look to encounters or material possession. While this is sometimes the case, the feeling of pleasure rarely lasts long.

Happiness is an art learnable. Rather than lying around, feeling the joy to come down upon you, or looking for satisfaction in all the wrong places, think about how you can integrate these keys into your life into real, lasting happiness.

1. Self-reliance.

You're a thing that's special to humanity. The soul is a blend of passions, talents, and quirks. If you don't show up as your true self to the world, just work in a way you feel like, you feel out of sync, and your levels of happiness will suffer.

2. Offer.

If you give without expecting anything in return from a place of love, you are nourished and satisfied just as much as your gift recipient is. Sharing doesn't have to be grandiose— you can give your heart a silent blessing, a kind word of encouragement, or a helping hand any time you see an opportunity.

3. Silence.

The modern world glorifies enterprise, and as a result, if you're like most people, you likely feel stressed and exhausted. The inner spirit needs time to rest, replenish, and refresh in peace and stillness. Consider meditating every morning for ten minutes and see what effect it has on your day and feelings of wellness.

4. Flow.

Flow is the feeling you get when you're lost in something you love. It could be to cook, write, paint, ride, create, serve others, or any number of things. You make a perfect place to be when you lose yourself in something that you enjoy— you understand your essential nature.

5. Thank you.

Gratitude is the sweet abbreviation for joy. It transforms what you have into enough; it trains your mind to reflect on all of the beauty, simple blessings, and goodness that surrounds you; and this provides you with feelings of happiness and enjoyment, which in turn makes you a magnet for more good things.

6. Awe.

A simple street, café, or park may seem fascinating and beautiful to our fresh eyes when we're on holiday in another city or country. Try to bring that same sense of awe to your local neighborhood and daily surroundings. The mysteries you discover can shock you.

7. Acknowledgment.

Eckhart Tolle teaches that our pain level depends on how responsive we are to the present moment. You simply accede to a sense of inner peace as you embrace the present moment as it is, thus freeing up your energy to make changes inside your control circle to create different outcomes for the future.

8. Presence.

Most of us are spending our lost days in our minds, dwelling on the past, or looking to the future. We don't communicate with life itself— with our senses, with our loved ones, the beauty of a sunrise, the sound of the breeze on our skin, or the taste of our breakfast. Try to connect the whole day to the present moment. It'll make your days feel a lot longer, lighter, and fuller.

9. Self-friendly.

The most meaningful friendship you will ever have is the one with yourself. Sadly, many of us are critical and contemptuous of ourselves. Start treating yourself as if you were addressing a best friend or loved one— with affection, kindness, and acceptance without condition. As the Buddha wrote, "You deserve your love and affection as much as anyone in the whole world."

10. Proposal.

The soul of everybody has one particular purpose in life. It may be a single great mission, or a series of smaller goals, such as enjoying earthly pleasures, helping others, and evolving into your own best version. Your path and purpose will be different from anybody else, so consult your own heart and intuition when making decisions about your life, instead of conforming to social norms.

11. Excellence.

There's a saying that says, "Worrying is like wishing for what you don't want." In most situations, worrying about the future is no more rational or reasonable than predicting a positive outcome— however, your life experience is likely to demonstrate that most things ultimately work out. So save yourself from the stressful, emotional turmoil, and develop an attitude based on hope, optimistic aspirations, and trust.

12. Work. Play.

A walk through the park on the way to a meeting seems like an obstacle, but for no reason whatsoever, a walk through the park looks like a pleasure and a privilege! Did you lose contact with the inherent playful spirit you had as a child? See if you can find it. Allow time to do things for enjoyment's sake, and add a positive attitude and play to your daily life and experiences.

13. Equilibrium.

We are taught in the ancient text The Tao Te Ching; there is a time for everything— a time for practice, and a time for rest, a time for certainty, and a time for uncertainty. Incorporate harmony into your life by mixing action times with rest periods. Reflect on whether your life is satisfying in all areas of life— from marriage, work, wellness, and learning, to money, leisure, and self-creation.

14. Compassion

We are all the same, and we are all equal on a fundamental level. You have a choice— to focus on the differences between yourself and others or to see the humanity you share in common. When you feel compassion for others and accept them as they are, you set yourself free— from other people's rigid expectations.

15. A whole new perspective.

A "miracle" is a change in our viewpoint about a person or situation— from feeling afraid to feeling secure and full of love; from grudging to practicing forgiveness; from getting upset by a trivial matter to understanding and letting go of the more exceptional picture of life. The more you put these changes into perspective, the more contentment and inner peace you'll feel.

Luck is relative. While others say performance, richness, and elegance do not describe what happiness is, those are all they need for some people. And you just can't impose on what makes people happy. If it's not a fleeting feeling of joy but a permanent source of happiness and contentment, it could be your true happiness.

So, how do you come across true happiness?

Chapter 5: Rediscover the actual values

The world is wrong, something fundamentally wrong and utterly wrong. We don't need to look too far for that to happen. The majority of people would agree to make that assertion. And when we stop contemplating the origin of the ills of our planet, a great deal comes to mind.

We start to wonder whether this is because we don't know enough. But this can't be so. Because we know more today as regards accumulated knowledge than men have known in any period of human history. We've got the facts available to us. We know more about mathematics, science, social science, and philosophy than we have ever known in any period in the history of the world. So it's not likely, because we don't know enough.'

And then we wonder whether this is because our scientific intelligence lags. If we have not made sufficient scientific progress, then. Well then, that may not be so. It has been fantastic for our scientific progress over the last few years. Man has been able to warp distance and place time in chains through his scientific genius, so that it is possible today to eat breakfast in New York City and dine in London, England. Back in about 1753, it took three days to go from New York City to Washington, and today, in less time than that, you can go from here to China. It cannot be that man's scientific progress is slow. The scientific genius of man was astonishing.

If we want to discover the exact cause of the problems of man and the real cause of the ills of the world today, we have to dig deeper than that. If we want to find it, then we will have to dig into men's hearts and minds.

The trouble is not that much we don't know enough, but it's as though we're not good enough. The problem is not so much;

our technological intelligence is lagging, but our spiritual genius is lagging. The significant problem facing modern man is that how we live has outstripped the spiritual ends we exist for. So we get caught up in a messed-up world. The problem lies with the soul of man himself and man. We didn't learn how to be just and honest, kind, genuine, and loving. And that is the very foundation of our problem. The real question is that we have made the world a neighborhood through our scientific genius, but we have failed to make it a brotherhood through our moral and spiritual inspiration. So today's great danger is not so much the atomic bomb that physical science has made. But the real threat facing civilization today is that nuclear bomb, which lies in men's hearts and souls, capable of exploding into the vilest of hatred and the most damaging egoism. That is the nuclear bomb that we have to fear today. The men are in trouble. Within human hearts and souls, that is the real groundwork for our issue.

5.1 What are the worldly and spiritual values?

Worldly Yet spiritual values in different directions seem to pull people. Look at each one in turn, and this becomes clear. How can one integrate them?

Worldly values concern mainly the basic human needs to survive and thrive: food, clothing, and shelter. It means not only ensuring that you can pay for what's needed, but also providing something extra for luxuries and health. The more worried you are about the threats and difficulties of life, the more likely you will want to benefit and accumulate.

It is a small leap from this status to one entirely encompassing monetary values, giving them a priority, if not the top. Anybody wants to be productive.

Besides wealth, power, and celebrity, priority is also given in a materialistic cultural environment. Never go hungry for the compelling need. Never do the prevalent need go without. We have more to live than they need, and they succeed. Those who are wealthy, reliable, and well-known may have more or less whatever they want, and this is not always good.

Then practical ideas, motivated by the desire for the benefit and the laws of supply and demand, are fundamentally mercenary. They are divisive, result in self-interest groups being developed, and place people in competition with each other. Some people say it's a benefit, but it can be destructive for both indignant winners and innocent losers.

Secular values are in no way guilty by themselves. They are right, but they decline quickly into being over-competitive, self-driven, and self-interested. We are initially need-driven and become readily greed-driven. We are filled with the fear of threatened insufficiencies with an urgency that ratchets the pace of life, imbued with a kind of disregard for anything but the short-term goal.

In comparison, spiritual values are of a more peaceful, everlasting nature, emerging from deep-seated inner relation to the divine or spiritual aspect of human experience. When maintained through daily prayer, meditation, and other spiritual practices, spiritual knowledge holds the real, spiritual self in contact and sync with the root of religious values, characterized by mature, selfless love.

From the list, the spiritual values then include:

Integrity

Confidence

Courtesy

Magnanimity

Tolerance

Patience

Persistence

Discrepancy

Humbleness

Courage

Body-Beauty

And that's Hope.

It's not sure if these are best understood as values or the virtues they are based upon. Either way, it's worth going through them slowly, spending quality time reflecting on each one's true meaning and significance.

It is also worth reflecting on how secular, materialist, worldly values can compete with and be distorted by these spiritual values. For example, complete honesty and unbounded kindness could well undermine the efforts of those who are involved in economic gain from advertising and selling products.

People may argue that the creation of wealth benefits all, and this can be true when considering only the material benefits. But when some are abused for the gain of others, personal ideals are undermined. Think of jobs in far-off places with low wages. Think too of customers who are motivated to spend on what might not be necessary for them, at the cost of more basic goods and services: not only food, clothing and shelter but health care and education as well.

There seems to be a dramatic conflict, but to reconcile human and moral ideals simply takes a formula: give priority to the latter at all times.

Even in the pursuit of earthly, apparently secular goals, spiritual values must predominate and prevail. This is the only antidote to depression and anxiety. Many of humanity's problems, conflict, misery, war, and famine among them, arise when the opposite happens when earthly ideals overpower spiritual sensibilities. This can be reversed, as human beings grow increasingly caring, knowledgeable, and educated, individually and ultimately collectively.

Humanity could be said to get through a sort of extended adolescence as we learn to take responsibility for the consequences of our personal and shared values governed by thoughts, words, and actions. This is the journey, the path, and the spiritual development pilgrimage on which we have each been since birth and in the course of life. It seems worth repeating that all of us are on that together.

If we are to move forward today, we must go back and rediscover some fundamental ideals that we have left behind. Only in this way can we make our world a better world and make the be what God wants it to be and its real purpose and meaning. The only way we can do this is to go back and rediscover those very positive ideals that we have left behind.

Often, you know, to move forward, you have to go backward. That's, that's, it's a working comparison.

Now that is what we have to do in today's world. We have left behind many valuable values; we have lost lots of useful benefits. So if we go forward, if we want to make this a happier world to live in, then we have to go back. We have to rediscover these important ideals which we have left behind.

The first is this— the first meaning theory we need to rediscover is this— that all truth rests on the moral foundations. In other words, this is a moral universe, and there are the universe's moral laws as compatible as the physical laws.

We, we never question that we must follow the physical laws of the universe. We have never doubted this. Even so, we just don't jump off aircraft or leap off high-rise buildings for the love of it — we don't. Since we know implicitly that there is a final rule of gravitation, and if you disobey it, you are going to suffer the consequences— we know. Even if in his Newtonian terminology we don't know it, we know it intuitively, and so we just don't fall off the highest building in Detroit for the fun of it — we, we, we don't. As we realize, there is a law of gravitation in the universe, which is final. Unless we disobey it, then we are going to suffer the consequences.

And then there is another thing, a second theory we have to go back and rediscover. And that is the spiritual control of all reality. In other words, we have to go back and rediscover the idea behind the cycle that there is a Creator.

Spiritualists and religionists believe that in one's life, there is a lack of deference to God and faith and that this is the source of addiction. Therefore, the idea is that placing greater emphasis on these aspects and allowing God more power over life would help to overcome the underlying issue.

Humans seek meaning in life. The reason for that may be different for everyone, but the common theme is the need for purpose. Many studies have shown that if a person focuses more on purpose in life, that intent has a positive influence on the outcomes of addiction treatment. Many people see having a higher force as being more excellent than themselves, giving them something to contribute to. For others, like me, the purpose is found in a greater good or calling, which drives everyday actions. Either way, looking at a larger picture can be a massive help to a successful recovery.

Spiritual development requires a connection to people, the universe, and meaning more significant than one's own. It may also embody values such as confidence, faith, respect, self-expression, and self-acceptance. These are precisely the things in the lives of many an addicted person who may be struggling with self-loathing and isolation that are necessary. But with a complex problem like addiction, a holistic approach that incorporates elements from all the camps, not just the field of spirituality and religion, is probably needed.

5.2 Shifting your focus to things that really matter

Do not hesitate to live in the best way you can every moment of your life because life is once, chances are small, and nothing is guaranteed - Blaze Olimady

Did you turn your attention away from what matters in life? It's not all about material wealth or the man, the women, the car and the home. Instead, it's about you, and once you start focusing on what matters, you can change other people's lives.

Every single emotion you feel can let you know more about the things in life that matter to you, and the things that don't matter.

Let's say you find that a friend of yours has thousands of followers when checking out Facebook or Instagram. Your emotional response to that piece of data in such a situation will tell you a lot about yourself.

If you have been insecure and felt terrible, you have to know you care about attention, recognition, or success. In other words, the incident influenced you mentally, because one of those things mattered to you.

It's not our iPhones, 3D TVs, brand new cars, or even our large and spectacular houses that are our most precious things.

You cannot find our most valuable resources at the bank. They're not available to order online. The fact is, they're on a concise list.

Our purpose, time, health, and our relationships are among our most precious commodities.

We live in a culture where external measures of success place a high premium. As a culture, we value appearances that match our unrealistic standards of beauty, pride ourselves on being always busy and seem continually striving to make more money or have more beautiful things. There's nothing wrong with being ambitious-but some of these outward successes are often wrongly equated with achieving greater happiness.

A miserable one today is not the set price for tomorrow's success. Even if you believe this is the happiness recipe, the brain instinctively knows it is not. That's why you're wasting your time on indulgences— the subconscious is trying to cheer something up.

Recovering from a substance use disorder may at first seem uncomfortable, yet finding and living a passionate life is a transformative way to rise above the grip of addiction.

Why does passion matter? Passion is the feeling that lends a spark to our mind.

Passionate about life keeps us engaged and active and gives us the motivation to live an authentic life. Understanding what ignites our spirit gives us not only a sense of joy but also a sense of purpose as a driving force.

1) Understand how to control your emotions: most people rarely pay attention to their emotional change unless they have severe feelings. Learn how to monitor your emotional changes for that can tell you a lot about yourself.

2) Find things that change your emotions: take note of it every time something changes your feelings. After a while, you'll have a list of things that change your beliefs• 3) Connect the dots: once you've got enough data, you'll find there's some trend that results in your attitudes shifting. If, for example, you feel bad about yourself when you see a successful person, then realize that your main goal in life is to succeed. It is just as plain as that.

Not only will your emotions help you understand yourself, but they'll also tell you what matters to you.

Here's the sad part. Most people ignore the signals their brains are sending them and even prefer to distract themselves not to notice them. Real happiness rarely happens until you start giving your mind the things that matter.

When you ignore the messages that your subconscious sends you, it'll reply back and forth by making you feel sad, down, and down.

Those bad emotions in such a situation are nothing more than stronger signals with the intent of inspiring you to pay attention to what matters.

Recognizing you have a problem can be the hardest step in recovery, but reading this is an excellent start in many ways, the fact you are here now.

You may have already tried to overcome the addictive behavior, but it was hard to keep up the momentum.

But don't give up no matter how many times you've tried before there's still hope-change is possible with the right attitude and support.

Regardless of the drug or behavior to which you are' addicted,' we agree that the key to beating addiction is not to concentrate on addiction, but on what life might be like for the non-addicted person.

Without trying to trivialize it, when you make your desire to use or act on your addiction, a secondary (and diminishing) element in your life, you overcome addiction–by clarifying, respecting, upholding, and living by the actual values that make you who you are.

To say that your beliefs affect your desire and ability to overcome addiction is to suggest that you are acting by what you believe in and care about.

They need to understand as a culture and as individuals that there is no more essential facilitator or solution to addiction than our beliefs. People who value clear thinking, for example, would shy away from regular intoxication. Likewise, a responsible person who is highly concerned about the wellbeing of his family would not encourage himself to shop or play away money from his family. People who concentrate on their health will be reluctant to drink excessively or refuse to take drugs.

Find absolute values that run counter to addiction you may discover inside yourself. Remember how much you value:

• Mindfulness and balance. Some people won't allow their lives to get out of control. We cannot picture themselves responding to some external stimuli automatically. Instead, they regulate their behavior by their values, principles, and ends. Such individuals may be repulsed, annoyed, or compassionate when they encounter someone else who drinks too much, or they are unable to deny more food assistance. You're reluctant to accept it in people near you.

• Completion and Expertise. Addiction is far less likely to hinder those who prioritize success and show life skills through their mastery and exercise. College students very rarely become addicted to cocaine and alcohol compared to poor people in the inner city, because they have other plans for themselves, which interfere with addictions. Though with the difficulty of student life and the small incentives, skills are exercised, and they look forward to more significant achievements. If you don't value success and don't see accomplishment in your future, the pre-eminent in removing addiction is to create the drive and the expectation that you can achieve meaningful goals.

• The self-awareness and knowledge of one's climate. Many people value alertness and sensitivity more than others. Such self-consciousness is painful for many drug addicts, and drugs are the best remedy for that pain. If a person strives to eradicate the suffering of consciousness, addiction will follow readily. The alternative is to value awareness and believe that such recognition pays off — that you'll get more out of it if you're awake to your environment. You are also less likely to become addicted if you have faith that thinking about a problem will lead to a solution, and blinding yourself to reality will get you into a deeper hole.

Health. What prevents most people from persisting in unhealthy addictions is the basic human instinct not to get hurt. On the other hand, some individuals do not care much that they harm themselves: that they are battered, that they destroy their lungs, or that their mental capacity is diminished. Telling a hard-drinking, hard-smoking, tattooed sailor (or a young drug and alcohol abuser in many cases) that his behavior is harmful often makes little impression. This is because, in his view, health is not a value to pursue and maintain. However, if your physical wellbeing is a personal priority for you, you are likely to abandon your addictive habits or moderate them.

• Self-esteem. Self-esteem protects you from addiction in two ways: first, by the need for permanent relief or consolation; second, by preventing yourself from being broken. Addictions and alcohol and drug abuse are like mini-suicide — killing yourself a bit every day. An adult tolerating being put down or beaten may feel that she has no right to reject those assaults. Those who lack that degree of self-hate are still not worth their value. And a natural outgrowth of this negative self-image is self-destructive behavior.

On the other hand, you can avoid addiction if you realize that hitting and putting down is wrong and that you deserve to be treated well. The more you trust yourself, the less addicted you want to be, and the less likely you are to become addicted to it.

• Connections with others, with the culture and with society. Most of those addictions are antisocial. We require, for example, an over-concentration on one's self and feelings. Habits are a kind of grim, twisted type of self-esteem — although they don't think about their wellbeing and wellbeing, abusers are so self-concerned that they harm others as much as they damage themselves or more. Addictions often demand that societal values be ignored. You're talking about people whose beliefs support the most damaging habits when you learn of a mother who locks her kids in the house while she goes out to score cocaine, or who locks up in her bedroom to get scrapped, or who prostitutes her kids; or of a father who spends all his money gambling, or who frequently falls drunk in front of his kids or beats them as well.

Such ideals are a kind of unrealized power that you can summon up: First of all, you're less likely to become addicted to the degree that you possess them and are more able to overcome the addictions that form.

5.3 Values Can Be a Conduit to Recovery

Your values are your belief that some things are right and good, some things are wrong and evil, some things are more important than others, and one way is better than another. Generally, beliefs are sincerely held — they come from your earliest experience and learning. Values represent what your parents have taught you, how much you have experienced in schools and religious institutions, and what the right and right social and cultural classes you belong to carry.

For all addictions, values are essential, not just addictive drinking and taking drugs. If you play, watch porn, or live your social media life compulsively to the exclusion of your' real life,' then your ideals are on show. The same principle applies to the enforcement of sexual opportunities that exclude productive activity. Most people enjoy sex, but because they feel it's wrong, they avoid compulsive or random sex. When you indulge in indiscriminate sex, then either you see a little mistake in it or the other principles in your life are less important than the good feelings that you derive from such sex. If you are willing to accept the laws, then so be it. On the other hand, if you have different beliefs that run counter to compulsive sexual activity, drinking, or shopping, then these values can be an essential tool for digging out your addiction.

Some people find alcohol incredibly soothing, sexually exhilarating, or some other strong feeling of welcome — but they don't become alcoholics. They refuse to go in there. If you have ever heard someone tell us, "I know that if I have more than one beer, I'll give the wind all the caution?" Most people who react to alcohol so violently say, "That is why I'm restricted to a single "or" drink, that's why I'm not drinking. "But alcoholics regularly override that realization about their reactions to alcohol and continue to drink.

Many principles contradict addictions directly. If you have those principles, they'll help you fight against addiction. And if you do not, it is a vital therapeutic resource to establish these principles. Declarations can convey values about what you think is right and wrong or your beliefs, such as:

• "I love our friendship"

• "I appreciate my wellbeing"

• "I believe in hard work"

• "Nothing is more important to me than my children"

• "It's humiliating to be out of reach with yourself" Certain values, or the lack of benefits, may reinforce addiction. For instance, if you don't think it's wrong to be drunk or high, if you don't care about fulfilling your commitments to other people, or if you don't care if you're productive at work, then you're more likely to be addicted.

First, identify your values, then rank the top three or five of them.

- Being with people
- Being loved
- Being married
- Having a special partner
- Having companionship
- Loving someone
- Having someone else's care
- Having a close family
- Having good friends
- Being popular
- Having people's approval
- Being treated justly
- Being admired
- Being independent
- Being brave
- Having things under control

Now describe a way to keep your focus on each of these values as leverage for changing your addiction.

Active addiction usually drives people away from their values, often light-years away. Practicing addicts often go against their own beliefs in ways that start as subtle but become more blatant overtime in their search to get what they want, be accepted by others, or either feel good or feel better. Sometimes it occurs within a couple of weeks, and sometimes it takes months or even years.

Still, no matter how optimistic and safe the ideals of an individual may be, those principles are inevitably overcome by the obsessive thinking of using alcohol and other drugs, the compulsive need to use them, and the self-absorbed behaviors that control active addiction.

• You may appreciate honesty, but if you would like to keep taking alcohol and other drugs to avoid the consequences, you have to be deceptive with your family, partner, employer, etc.

• You may appreciate responsibility, but the nature of active addiction leaves you gradually less likely to act responsibly.

• You can enjoy education and want a college or higher degree, but using alcohol and other drugs stopped you from continuing or completing your studies.

• You can value being safe and physically fit, but it's becoming less and less important because of active addiction.

As the active addiction progresses, most people drift further and further away, even from the values they hold most closely. We consider themselves to be people we never thought they were going to be and they don't want to be, they never imagined they would lead such lives and doing things they never thought they'd. If what you do and how you behave is contradictory to your beliefs, it is creating frustration, remorse, and unhappiness. That is a source of immense guilt and shame for many people. This pain can also be right, as distressing and painful as the pain caused by acting in ways that contradict the beliefs can be — it can inspire improvement.

Addiction includes consuming alcohol and other drugs to make you feel good or better— it is about finding gratification through neurochemical reinforcement and relaxation. However, the way to genuine happiness and contentment is not through pleasurable experiences that rely on external circumstances. It's an inside job, just like recovery. This comes from making safe, supportive decisions that match our beliefs. If our acts are consistent with our expectations, we engage in life in a way that we can feel good about, irrespective of the external conditions. Conversely, it is almost impossible to feel positive about ourselves when our actions contradict our values— no matter what the result of external circumstances may be.

Once you understand that, you know that what's most important about how you live your life is because it is the source of pure contentment. When the actions of people uphold their beliefs, they do the right thing— regardless of criticism or praise, suffering or happiness, loss, or benefit. And they still feel far better about themselves, in turn.

But to act in such a way as to honor your values, you need to recognize the values you hold. When was the last time you were talking about your benefits? Some people do not do this unless they are shaken up by a significant event (usually an extremely cynical, painful or traumatic experience) so much that they feel compelled to rethink the meaning and purpose of their lives. When that happens, a crisis can become a chance to think deeply about what their ideals are and whatever kind of life they would like to lead. Coming to that place where people are in addiction treatment can be a crisis that creates such an opportunity. The problem then becomes, how are they going to use that?

It is not uncommon for them to change over time, even though values are often relatively stable. When we move through life and experience new and different things, some ideas become less important to us, while others become more so. That is one reason why daily consideration of what matters to you is beneficial and safe. Even if you think your beliefs haven't changed over the years, engaging in the practice of clarification of values is still helpful.

As a result, people always experience some changes in their values when they move from active addiction to recovery. Long-standing values that people have ignored or let slide again become a priority during their addiction, while some newer benefits may also begin to take on significance. Recovery provides an opportunity to identify and set new positive goals and reinvigorate the personal qualities to which alcohol and other substance use have always been relevant but buried.

Just as what changes are essential to you, so does your definition of success — and your values. That is why it is a lifelong practice to remain in constant touch with your beliefs, but it is particularly valuable to participate in them now.

Recovery allows you to regroup and to rediscover what matters in life. When you have lost all that is material, there is still the spiritual aspect of healing that is linked to your soul, and that's what holistic therapy is all about. You will rediscover what matters to you, psychologically speaking, through reflection, instruction, and counseling, and a professional holistic therapist can help you create a new life based on your beliefs that nothing can take away from you.

5.4 Live a meaningful life

Some views of addiction, as you already know, assert that people cannot change their addicted identities. But it's also important to note that improving one's self-image is challenging for all types of people, not just former drug addicts or alcoholics. Body images of people, for example, are very persistent. So people who have been fat since childhood tend to see themselves as they always have been-even after weight loss.

You can believe your addiction is still on fragile ground. You may choose to abstain from alcohol, avoid opportunities for casual sexual contact, or deliberately avoid buffets. But you don't need to think of yourself as an addicted person anymore.

Leading a lifetime, not paying attention to your addiction, and not visualizing the self-addict in every situation are all ways of creating your new identity. There are drawbacks of knowing that you are not an addict, and thus exposing yourself to others. Your recognition of your non-addict self-image will strengthen your new self-view just as your confidence in your new identity will persuade others of its truthfulness.

If you've become secure enough to look outward to other people and expand the scope of your life— to be a more productive, healthier person, a better friend and parent, a better member of the community— then you're prepared to set yourself broader goals.

You also grow to be someone working to create a better world for yourself and others.

Your addiction problems have been the product of choices, and the road to a new life will also be the result of choices. Always determine your chosen path.

Living a life of purpose is one of the most important ways for those in recovery to maintain their sobriety so that they are motivated to avoid relapse.

What is your purpose?

Our intention is why. It is what drives our actions. It is fueling our fire. This includes our jobs, our relationships, and the way we live our lives. It wraps everything that we do around it. This means a deliberate way of living our lives. It brings a sharper focus to our lives.

That keeps us going when life gets tough is our why.

Our why gives extra meaning and wealth to live.

If we have lost our way and struggle with our cause, we should ask ourselves a few related questions:

- Where am I trying to get to?

- What is it that lights me up and excites me?

- What's my motivation to get up in the morning?

- What more do I want in my life?

- What, in my life, do I want less?

The responses can be insightful to these questions and can bring us back to the core of what matters most to us. Listen to and use these answers as guiding light. Revisit them often. Many people lose connection with their true selves during an addiction. Think about yourself before you get into the habit. It takes a couple of minutes to recall the person you were. Where are you from? Who'd you hang out with? What was your thing to do? Who woke you up before your addiction?

You have dramatically changed from the person that you once were. You've learned hard lessons, but for that, you're a better, wiser person. However, interacting mentally with the person you once were will help you remember things you were excited about once gave you excitement. What have your goals and ambitions been? Are those goals still of interest to you? Or will the new one forge you an original path?

What do you feel passionate about now? What do you think is important now?

Allow time to write down new goals, aspirations, and desires. Use this list to start mapping yourself out a function.

Even if you don't have a particular purpose in mind right now, there are fundamentals all can gain from reflecting on.

Wellbeing and exercise. So many of us take for granted our wellbeing until we have justification not.

We ignore exercise and then wonder why our bodies suffer when we have to climb a stepping stone route. We are neglecting our diet and then asking when all this extra weight is creeping over us. We are neglecting our mental health and then asking why we always get depressed.

We can be more childlike on ourselves. We should integrate daily movement into our lives. Walking, gymnastics, bodyweight workouts, yoga— everything counts, and all can be combined. Our bodies are made to move all day, not idle humped over computers or in front of televisions. Embrace movement capability.

Healthy eating can be easy and enjoyable too. We should base the majority of our food on plants (fruits and vegetables). When we eat meat, we will view it as a side dish and ensure that a variety of vegetables fills the majority of the rest of our plates. Few foods need to be off-limits, and the occasional choice we can still make room for. Eating healthy can and should be fun, and should never feel like drudgery.

Being more outside, sleeping healthy, and taking time to decompress can all improve our mental health and wellbeing of feelings. We can be more patient with ourselves by making sure that we occasionally make time to reset.

Routine check-ups with our physicians will help to gather early signs of something wrong, but we can also do our utmost to make the most of what we have by doing our best to care for ourselves.

Physical exercise is a great way to get your emotions, health, and life under control. Use affects your mood tremendously, and also has a psychological effect on you. Taking control of your health will make you feel more in control of the whole of your life. You will make better choices if you are in charge. So you won't be influenced by others too quickly.

Spirituality. People often confuse faith with spirituality. Religious practice can often be a great way of finding a spiritual path, but the two need not go hand in hand. If you have religious roots, you find fulfilling; this is now an excellent time to reconnect with it.

If you don't have religious roots, you can still spiritually start developing yourself. Spirituality simply means going beyond human survival's simple thoughts and actions to tap into something higher. Your soul is an essential part of yourself. The soul can help us make better and better choices for ourselves. Since many people ignore their spirit, though, it's easy to forget that it is even there.

By learning more about it, you can start care for your soul. Read books on spirituality, and how to connect better with your soul. Take some time to be alone and still every day. You may not be ready to start meditating just yet, but always take the time with yourself to be alone. Pray, reflect, revue. This is even a spiritual practice that will allow you to reconnect with your soul.

Helping others. A tremendous learning opportunity you've just come through. You're on the other side, now. You are smarter, and you are wiser. You have so many people around you who can profit from the newly found strength and wisdom.

Some of the great things you will do is helping others to give meaning to your life. When we go beyond ourselves and start focusing on others, we work at the highest level. Such types of activities will increase your motivation, your drive, your concentration, and your intent.

There is a myriad of ways to help. Think of something you're passionate about and then look for opportunities to volunteer in that field.

Maintaining your accountability relationships will help you keep track of your new life of intent. Accountability doesn't just apply to those who complete rehab. Responsibility is essential for everyone to make personal enhancements and build community.

All of us are responsible. If we keep a sense of accountability constant, we'll want to be our best for our friends, family, and community members. Don't stop reckoning. The moment you begin to reject responsibility, you change your course.

It's hard to recover, but you've come a long way. Now, you are better. Now you're smarter. You're ready to take on a purposeful life that will keep you rising and healing.

Relationships. Our current fixation with being busy causes many of us to believe that in our days we are not getting enough time. This is an especially sorry state of affairs when it means our relationships are "not given time."

The truth is, all this busyness might just be something we made with a hand. While this may not be welcome news, it does mean that we can also step back from it and live a different way.

What brings life to our lives are our friends, family, and loved ones. We have to take the time to foster these relationships. It's fine to be busy if we're busy with the things and people that mean us the most.

Our relationships are our foundation and our bedrock. We need to foster them with their due love and attention.

Purpose, time, wellbeing, and those who cherished them are the things that make us more productive and fuller. Let's handle them accordingly.

Make every moment significant.

All too often, we feel bitter about the past or worry about what may happen in the future. We either express regrets or are worried. The reality is, it's just now. Only at this moment can you live— that's why you need to make this moment count. What has happened has passed, and it depends on what you are doing right now. Make every moment significant.

Be happy now since joy is not destiny.

Learn to take advantage of every minute of your life. Now remain happy. Don't expect anything outside yourself to make you happy in the future. Consider how precious the time you have to spend, whether at work or with your kids, really is. It should be enjoyed and savored every minute. Earl Nightingale

Live for the moment when you can be as content as you can. Realize that when you have done something, you do not have to be happy. Happiness is something you choose, a state of mind that attracts more things to be pleased about!

Find your authenticity by searching for who you indeed are.

Who are you, then? -are you fighting for? Discovering your authentic self is up to you. Only then do you become home. Free to be bold, blaze your trail, and say what you are thinking without conforming to other people's ideas. Look at your values: they'll remind you what you're here for.

Deeply love, give & share with others.

Feeling deeply loved by someone gives you energy while being genuinely in love with someone gives you courage. Lao

Tzu Love yourself first. You will genuinely love someone else only when you know your true worth. Practice day today, self-love. Pick some beautiful things for yourself. Look in the mirror and say good things to yourself. At first, it may sound a little different, but you're going to get used to it. Self-love lets you love others.

What matters most is your perceptions.

Life aims to live it, to taste experience to the fullest, to reach out for newer and richer experiences with eagerness and without fear. Eleanor Roosevelt Their real-life experiences matter. Which perceptions are you making to yourself? Allow time to experience unforgettable experiences that will light you up. You are here, so make it count for the ultimate life experience.

Everything is about interest.

Your convictions become your emotions; your feelings become your actions; your words become your acts; your deeds become your practices; your behaviors become your principles; your values become your destiny. Mahatma Gandhi, What beliefs do you hold? Identify them every day and obey them. They will not only enable you to make the right decisions, but authenticity and confidence come out of your values to shine and be who you are with integrity. You can be truthful to yourself and others.

Chapter 6: Self-Awareness through Self Observation

Being self-conscious involves being mindful of your emotions, intentions, behaviors, thoughts, and feelings. It can be knowing the reasons for substance use, for example, rather than living in denial about your addiction. Self-awareness may also include knowledge of the causes, such as certain feelings, circumstances, or individuals, that contribute to your drug use. This knowledge helps you to take control of these attitudes, opinions, and events, allowing you to make changes in your life. Additionally, self-awareness is seen as a self-control mechanism, an essential tool in treating addiction.

Addiction affects how we see ourselves, and in effect, destroys a degree of our self-awareness. We cannot observe and evaluate our emotions, motivations, and behaviors accurately anymore. For example, many people fighting addiction deny they have a substance abuse problem. Denial is an enormous factor that contributes to a lack of self-awareness, which encourages the ongoing use of drugs and alcohol, preventing successful rehabilitation.

To support addiction treatment and facilitate full recovery, self-awareness can be improved and developed. The notice of your habits and patterns is an essential step toward improving self-awareness. In this case, specifically, those patterns that lead to your use of the drug. Becoming more aware of these patterns enables you to change them and stop the use of drugs before they start. The response to "Pause and Prepare" is often used as a method to become more conscious of and resolve one's habits when appropriate. The reaction to "Pause and Plan" consists of pausing before acting, assessing the situation critically, and planning your answer carefully. The hope when using this technique is that implicit habits of thought that have historically led to drug use will be objectively analyzed and reversed in favor of more favorable outcomes. This allows you to become aware of the situation and respond appropriately, allowing your decisions to be aligned with your values and goals.

Your negative thinking habits are becoming conscious of another phase in achieving self-awareness. This can be achieved by tracking your "self-talk" and asking questions like "What is my inner dialog?" Is that true?" Does it influence how I behave in certain circumstances or how I feel?" And how can this be changed?". You can address any false hypotheses or convictions that you may hold through this method. Drug use may occur, for example, because you are lonely, and feel that the only way to make new friends is to take drugs with fellow drug users. It, of course, is not accurate, and you will be able to address its false belief by tracking and objectively analyzing your self-talk.

Self-awareness and drug addiction are strongly linked together. While addiction can strip away our self-consciousness, building it allows for a lasting recovery to be achieved.

6.1 The relevance of the Self-observation

Self-awareness occurs when a person knows himself and, in particular, ways why he thinks, feels, and behaves. It is the opposite of denial that occurs when a person in his life denies or avoids challenging and troublesome thoughts, feelings, and behaviors. It is not easy to move past denial and into a state of healthy self-awareness, it is a critical component of any kind of positive self-improvement.

Then there are the sensitivity factors that a person can concentrate on: • Feelings: learning to recognize and mark feelings as clearly as possible will help an individual become more conscious of what they feel in a given situation.

• Patterns: any events, emotions, thoughts, or feelings that occur frequently should be examined and discussed to help the person understand the reasons for feeling and behaving in some ways.

• Sensations: anything a person feels physically should be assessed to other things so that they can better understand how their body reacts physically to activities, feelings, and thoughts.

• Thoughts: the individual needs to understand what goes through his mind, what ideas and beliefs dominate his dreams, and how his inner monolog affects his emotions and behaviors.

Self-awareness is about having a clear view of all things, from strengths and weaknesses to desires and feelings to your personality. This allows us to understand other people's opinions and motivations, how we're viewed, and the logic behind our attitudes. The ability to do these things is essential to know or to "find ourselves" We achieve inner peace by understanding who we are, and can control our mental wellbeing effectively. Self-awareness contributes to active rather than the passive living of a life.

It we are not self-conscious, we often fall victim to prejudice in affirmation, the propensity to view new evidence as proof of existing beliefs or theories. For instance, if we have a strong dislike of someone, then we are likely to interpret events— even those where that particular person displays desirable characteristics— as an intruder to their identity as a "rotten individual." The same can be said of ourselves, "I know that I am the right person, and those good people are not getting addicted. And I can't be an abuser. We have psychological tendencies to accept only incomplete representations of ourselves, and this sort of prejudice is what led them to years of substance abuse.

It's natural to look for knowledge when you know something or think you do something to validate that belief. Instead of looking constructively at instances as autonomous, we use them to reinforce our current views. The ability to recognize our motivations and desires independently from our personality is self-consciousness. Part of what makes this so challenging is that we see ourselves through the same fixed lens that we expect others to be viewing who we are. The reason this is an issue is that our interpretation of events and circumstances has a duality to it. Too often in life, we see these things as good or bad, happy or sad, and positive or negative without allowing us to see them simply as they are through an unbiased lens.

Addiction has a fascinating connection to self-confidence. People generally have a reason to use drugs, and for a multitude of reasons, addicts use them. They range from mental illness and trauma masking to just trying to get high. It becomes intuitive or unconscious to some (addicts), while self-awareness requires contemplation and thinking.

That is part of the reason why it is so vital to postpone exposure to addictive substances until age 21. It's because, over time, we develop self-awareness. Their brain development (which involves self-awareness, among other things) comes to a halt when the use begins at an early age.

Although addiction frequently starts as an attempt to find relief, addicts often lack an understanding of themselves — the consequence of conceding to our own biases. Biologically speaking, the lowest effort for the greatest reward is equal to a good outcome. It perpetuates the problem, which is further compounded by the fact that drugs reduce the amount of dopamine, serotonin, and endorphins (pleasure chemicals) our brain naturally generates. The feeling that a biological need is going unmet is what ends up happening.

Every individual who is addicted to drugs or alcohol has his or her self-confidence robbed. He or she wanders into a vacuum where feelings are out of balance, trust is lost, and strengths and weaknesses cancel out each other. The addict has nothing left to stop a life that spirals out of control. Recovery of self-awareness in addiction is required to understand personal power, set goals, and effectively communicate.

Lack of self-awareness causes an addict's life to be negatively impacted and destroys his or her ability to focus on growth and where he is going. There is no power over feelings and no real inner strength to rely upon. The addict will rarely look past his or her next drug or beverage. Self-awareness in addiction recovery is a necessary life skill to set goals and prevent relapse, according to the (SAMHSA) Substance Abuse and Mental Health Services Administration. Without self-consciousness, the addict is unaware of the dangers physically as well as mentally ahead. Self-awareness in addiction recovery is a critical ingredient in the formula for a better life, with less chance of recurrence down the road.

Restoring self-awareness provides the addict with the following tools for his or her recovery:

• Establishing and achieving goals

• Maintaining successful relationships

• Recognizing strengths and shortcomings

• Doing instead of responding

• Establishing a belief system

• Controlling their actions

• Navigating issues recovery does not mean that life will be perfect because there is no such thing, but it strengthens the recovering additive.

Self-consciousness means the person knows who they are and what they want out of life.

Becoming more self-conscious is an arduous process. The success depends on your willingness to change and your receptivity. How can they get you started? Such starting steps can include enhancing your self-awareness to recognize and avoid relapse triggers:

1. Put the time in. You can find the behavior patterns apparent by spending time in self-reflection or asking thoughtful questions. You might find, for example, that you choose to use your drug-of-choice around certain people and places or in particular situations. Understanding this can allow you to recognize the causes, and you know that you need to avoid specific interactions and settings.

2. Beware of your physical responses and reactions. Physical reactions such as rapid heartbeat, stomach ache, tensed shoulders, and muscles, or headache can be early signs of an emotional response to a stressful situation. Such symptoms can be used as an early warning system to avoid a relapse.

3. Comprise the feelings. Identifying and labeling your emotions and recognizing their source is an essential part of recuperating addiction. Instead of running away from your beliefs, be open with them and take in what they tell you. Is your frustration a reaction to stress? Would you feel sad, just because you have some disturbing news? Whatever you think, know it's going to pass, and your feeling has a source. This way, you can put a healthy response in the strategies.

4. Think back on your tastes. Pensées also precede acts. So if you watch your emotions, you will notice negative patterns of thought. What do you say yourself continuously in your

mind? Tell yourself you aren't good enough internally (this is very common)? Say to yourself you're stupid? Laughter? Wordless? Don't believe the thinking! Negative thinking is, in essence, a pattern-a script-created and reinforced by the environment. Once you disconnect and start taking control of your emotions, you can make some destructive actions easier to forestall. You can change your thinking and create a new outcome!

5. Demand reviews. Feedback from others will help you identify your blind spots and strengthen your actions in the future. During family therapy sessions or in group counseling sessions, you may receive feedback from loved ones. And, if you find you spiraling down, ask a close friend or partner to say a "safe word." Often perspective can help!

Only 10 examples of the many ways in which sober living can make your life better.

1. Good partnerships.

When you are sober, then you will be able to form and sustain healthier relationships. If you're a parent, this is an incredible place where sober living will profoundly affect your life and those around you. Rebuilding healthy relationships with your kids may take some time, but you will no doubt be a more compassionate, more attentive, and more optimistic parent.

You'll become a better friend too. You'll have more time to build meaningful relationships, plus you'll likely become more trustworthy and honest. As you become acquainted with yourself in recovery, you will know what kind of things you are interested in and will find friends who enjoy the same. Sober friendships are potentially the most uplifting and rewarding relationships you've ever had.

2. The memory is growing.

You are no more missing out on important events, like the birthdays of your children. No more to wake up full of shame and remorse when you wonder what happened the previous night. You get to remember everything when you are living sober. You are more mindful of the finer details of life— like a smile from a stranger or a freshly flowered flower. Besides, being sober will allow you the clarity of mind to reveal your interests and achieve your goals.

3. You're looking much better.

If you avoid using chemicals to kill your body, your skin will naturally look better. Clear blemishes, wrinkles lose some of their meaning, minimizing dark circles. Many people find they look ten years younger until they start living soberly. But the benefit is not trivial. If we look better, we inevitably feel better about ourselves. Sometimes, all the other rewards of a sober life will have you smiling more— which will keep you looking great.

4. It would be best if you kept your weight safe.

Some mention initial weight management as a benefit to living soberly in recovery. You naturally lose weight when you stop consuming empty alcohol calories and engage in drunken binge-eating episodes. If you were underweight due to a condition of substance abuse, your weight is also likely to return once sober to a healthy level. This will help you feel physically better and reduce your risk of health complications related to pressure.

3. You've got more money.

Living sober will leave you with the extra money you would otherwise waste on feeding your drug or alcohol addiction. This is an automated strategy to save money. You can pay off debts with more capital, save on more significant purchases, and invest in new hobbies. Instead of continually emptying your bank account and having nothing to show, you can now spend your money acquiring meaningful experience with people who love you and care about you.

6. You've got more time.

You probably didn't realize exactly how much time you spent thinking about and drug and alcohol use until you stopped. It can be frustrating at first to have all this extra time and leave you with no idea what to do. It does not take long to realize, but once you're sober, there's a lot of things to do. You might use your energy to go about things like walking your dogs, visiting family and friends, learning something new, and having more sleep— all of which turns out to be much more satisfying than getting drunk or high.

7. They've got more energy.

Feeling constantly tired from the quality of sub-par sleep is a thing of the past. While it may be hard at first sleep as your body adjusts, once you're sober, you'll find your rest is of higher quality, and you'll get more of it. Plus, your body won't have to work so hard to repair the damage of drug and alcohol abuse, freeing up the energy resources available to it. Who wouldn't want to have more funds in one day? Sobriety gives you that.

8. You're having more fun.

Sure, you'll have more fun living soberly than intoxicated (although at first, it doesn't seem that way). With more time, money, and energy, fun opportunities are endless and never require a hangover. Your definition of fun is likely to change for the better, and finally, you're going to think to yourself, "how have I ever thought life like that was enjoyable? "When sober, you're able to play more, when your happiness is real, you'll have a youthful radiance, and you can appreciate the daily life experience.

9. You have earned respect.

You gain respect from others when you are sober because they understand your commitment to change. Through volunteering and supporting others, you make a good impression on the people around you. People are looking up to you and smiling at your sobriety. You can follow through with commitments when you are sober, and people will start to trust you again. To become sober is an excellent display of self-respect as you commit to stop abusing your body and mind — and you are more likely to be recognized by people too when you respect yourself.

10. You feel alright about yourself.

Feeling better about yourself is one of the best presents of sobriety you will be having. First of all, you can get rid of the shame and guilt that is linked to your addictive behavior. You can be proud of yourself every day to make it another day in recovery. While it will also take some work to increase your self-esteem and not just happen overnight after you recover, living sober will lead to long-term healthy self-esteem.

6.2 Negative emotions and their role in addiction

Humans are emotional beings, and in a single day, they can all be sad, happy, grumpy, excited, anxious, and terrified. Emotions are unstable and temporary. Those who are struggling with addiction tend to grab a negative emotion as if it were a permanent condition, and he or she can never get rid of the feeling. We become discouraged when an addict feels a positive emotion because it doesn't last. Recovery of feelings and addiction requires the momentary recognition of the sensation and realizing it is temporary. Understanding to understand and control the daily-appearing emotions is a fundamental principle in the recovery process.

The words "emotions" and "feel" are commonly used interchangeably. Strictly speaking, between those two words, there is a distinction. Emotions refer to a state of thinking that occurs to something that happens. A feeling can contain several different sentiments. The feeling of love would be an excellent example of this consisting of the opinions of happiness and trust.

Early sobriety is often described as an emotional ride on a rollercoaster. It refers to how people can experience these highs and lows from day to day–sometimes even an hour to hour. Such emotional swings tend to settle down after a few months of sobering people but may continue to be a problem for many years.

Dealing with feelings can be a recuperating test for people. If they don't do that well, it can mean that their sobriety is at risk. The emotions that are most likely to cause people problems to include:* Loneliness* Anger* Fear* Disappointment* Guilt* Boredom* Excessive joy–pink cloud syndrome Individuals turn to drug misuse and alcohol abuse for some different reasons. Some of the fundamental emotions driving and managing substance use disorder is often related to what psychologists label as having a negative or negative effect.

A negative effect is a psychological term that identifies emotions or emotional states linked to depression and often contributes to individuals devaluing themselves. Individuals experiencing adverse effects may also engage in many perceptual distortions or misunderstandings about themselves, others, and the world that may interfere with their functioning. Depression and rage are two adverse affective conditions that can significantly interfere with the recovery from a substance use disorder.

When you listen to what they're saying, negative emotions can be a catalyst for development. On the other hand, negative thinking leads to talking to yourself about giving up. Feeling inferior is a warning to evaluate your objectives and what you need to change to achieve them: but if you respond by deliberately telling yourself, "I'm not successful, I'm still going to be a failure," you'll soon have little left but self-pity and depression— and maybe recur to addiction.

Letting go of negative thoughts is necessary, but that doesn't mean battling or avoiding them— the approach often only makes them stronger. Let the words roll on and off your brain as you bring positive facts to replace them: "I think I can do that. Before I have overcome obstacles, and I'm going to succeed again. "The ability to process your feelings is an essential part of recovery. But many addicted young men have learned to numb their emotions, making a comeback from craving all the more complicated.

A lot of us were taught from a very young age that so-called' bad' emotions such as sadness and anger are unacceptable-especially for men, which leads many young men to suppress their emotional responses or even reject them outright. But the fact is, in the light of addiction recovery, manipulating the feelings is neither safe nor advisable.

Recovery can be robust by the desire to suppress emotion. This is because successful recovery also involves coping with the emotional issues that first contributed to drug or alcohol abuse. You may want to be genuinely free from addiction without a healthy dose of emotional honesty, but find out you're unfit to do it.

The recovery process is often an emotional process beyond that. Dramatic changes in life will leave you feeling lonely and isolated. Meanwhile, signs of withdrawal will affect the brain physiologically-and; thus, your mental and emotional condition. In early recovery, many people also feel a surge of emotions when they come to terms with their past actions and the effects they have had on those they care about.

For some people, an emotional rollercoaster is an early recovery. It's a critical step to learn to handle and cope with those emotions. Yet as we'll see in this article, it's one that is challenging for many young men who struggle with addiction to master–if that sounds familiar to you, you're not alone.

These are much more likely to try to flee when men struggle to communicate or even understand their emotions. This can aid in a wide range of issues, such as:

- Abuse of drugs and alcohol

- Anger

- Aggression

- Thrill-seeking actions

- Workaholism

- Compulsive sex

- Psychosomatic disorders

 And these are just a few potential problems that may occur. Not only can emotional avoidance lead to self-destructive habits, such as substance abuse or compulsive behavior, but the actions it produces can also exacerbate this. It leads to a self-defeating process, which can be very difficult to overcome for a young man with mental insecurities.

Emotions and drug use are strongly related. Many people start using psychoactive drugs because of the euphoric or soothing feelings they can produce. People choose to involve in alcohol and drugs to cope with a stressful day, bad news, or when they are depressed or socially anxious, to make them feel accepted.

Drugs and alcohol often switch from being an occasional means of stress relief for many regular users to being an essential part of their ability to cope with difficult emotions. Positive experiences and excitement can also trigger the urge to use them, with people turning to substances to celebrate important milestones and at exciting events such as concerts, parties, and sporting games.

Feelings often take up a back seat to use throughout addiction. Many users are unable to take care of their emotional needs when coping with addiction's turmoil and uncertainty, and the constant cravings to be used. This often results in periods of extreme emotional self-neglect, where an addict can begin to feel lonely, disconnected, and disengaged from the outside world.

When you begin to take care of your emotional needs in sobriety again, feelings and emotions that you may have dulled for many years start to reemerge. Throughout early recovery, happiness, sorrow, compassion, and empathy are usually felt throughout new ways that can be both exhilarating and daunting. You will also likely experience many individuals, places, and emotions in early recovery that has mental associations with drugs and alcohol, and may cause the desire to use them.

It can be challenging to deal with negative feelings and experiences, which is why a lot of people turn to drugs and alcohol to cope. Substance abuse offers an escape, rather than facing these painful feelings. This can be something of self-medication or a way of masking fact, but the misuse of drugs does not provide the help that a person truly needs to overcome difficult emotions. Using drugs or alcohol can worsen the experience of an individual and trigger negative emotions.

One of the hardest parts of healing is its emotional aspect. Even if you can help someone abstain physically from substance abuse, it is harder to deal with the underlying issues that drive its continuation. A person can easily get overwhelmed by what surfaces without the help of substances to stifle the impact of emotional difficulties. Immediately, they face negative feelings; they don't know how to handle healthily. Some of these feelings are triggered by the loss of drugs and signs of withdrawal, while others are thoughts that initially led to the development of addiction. Whatever order they have grown in, dealing with feelings healthily is key to a successful recovery.

Emotions can trigger substance abuse, so learning new ways to cope with them is imperative. You will better prepare for potential pitfalls of treatment by knowing what feelings you associate with substance abuse. Some of the most common emotions felt and related to violence and withdrawal of drugs include

1. Anxiety: Substance abuse is a common trigger. Substances are commonly used to relieve anxiety symptoms and to help people communicate with others. Sadly, it may also cause anxiety to increase until substance abuse ends. Just thinking about being unable to use will cause anxiety symptoms to surface.

2. Depression: Substances are often misused to treat depression symptoms for self-medication. Use can cause euphoria, and many people are chasing the high substances that are creating. Drugs and alcohol can alter the functioning of the brain, which makes abstinence much harder. Depression is generally felt during withdrawal and, when not appropriately treated, can lead to a plethora of issues.

3. Paranoia: The act of drug abuse or alcohol itself can cause insanity. The fear of being caught, substance abuse induces the feeling that people around you are conspiring against you or communicating behind your back and a vague sense of dread. It is possible to experience those same emotions while going through withdrawal. Even in rehabilitation, anxiety is a common side effect.

4. Nervousness: Fear is a collective experience because of the way drugs and alcohol influence your brain chemistry. Similar to anxiety and paranoia, when you think about going forward without drugs as a crutch, many people experience terror.

5. Frustration: Several aspects of a person's experience can cause failure. Rage could be a side effect of drug abuse, but it is also part of the withdrawal process to become irritable and experience mood swings. You can perceive frustration more clearly and more frequently without substances clouding your thoughts or memories. Anger can be motivated by emotions about being in recovery, dwelling on past actions and behaviors, or knowing that drugs or alcohol can no longer be used.

6. Disappointment: Another common emotion in rehabilitation is deceit. You would be dismayed that you can't use drugs any more, but when you reflect on the past, you may also feel regret. In a sober mind, past actions and behaviors can produce sensations of disappointment.

7. Loneliness: Besides losing your favorite drug, you often neglect relationships with friends who misuse the substance. Although recovery needs this phase, it can still leave you feeling lonely. Loneliness can be a driving force for substance abuse development and can be a powerful emotion in recovery. **Once recovering from dependency**, it is essential to develop healthy relationships.

 8. Guilt: Guilt can be a robust emotion to deal with in recovery, much like a disappointment. It can cause intense feelings of guilt to look back on past decisions, actions, and behaviors. Once your mind starts clearing up, you might start feeling more guilty about how drugs have made you communicate with others.

9. Resentment: Even if you know therapy is the right course of action, jealousy can still be a strong feeling, especially in early recovery. It applies above all to all who were involuntarily forced into care. It can take up to a person a while he **gets to grips** with resentment feelings but it's a normal response to life-changing action.

10. Boredom: The boredom can be a relapse risk factor. Most people find themselves in their pockets with much more energy to occupy their time without substance abuse. Boredom can cause a person to reconsider using drugs or alcohol, making a recovery a particularly problematic feeling. Planning and arranging to fill up as much time as possible will help minimize this risk.

6.3 How to face negativity and embrace it

Emotions, by themselves, are perfectly understandable reactions to circumstances. The advantage of negative emotions is that they provide you with an opportunity to step back and reassess the situation. Active addiction, however, has roots in a desire to avoid having to cope with fear, anger, sadness, or heartbreak.

Most addictions make a way of living emotional numbness. When emotions start flooding back after you're sober again, it can be overwhelming and must confront them without drug or alcohol cr. Do not multiply the issues by focusing on why you "shouldn't" feel some way. Find a positive outlet for dealing with your emotions and talk to a therapist or supportive loved one about your feelings, concerns, and desires.

It takes practice to learn how to cope with these emotional triggers, without turning to the common effects of drugs and alcohol. Positive self-care and working on some necessary emotional wellness skills can create a safety net where you can learn to experience your feelings more comfortably and overcome the triggers you need to use.

Here are a few approaches to support.

Try to become conscious of your emotions first. Just being able to stop and think about your feelings as they happen can lessen their effect on you. Being able to see your feelings as they come, placing a mark on them, and acknowledging their short term presence in your mind and body provides you with a chance. To determine how to react to your feelings, rather than falling prey to the involuntary thoughts and behaviors that they can cause. Being aware and respectful of your opinions as they come and go puts you back in the driver's seat and gives you options on how to react. Keeping your thoughts and triggers journal can help you become more aware of your overall patterns and also track progress.

Second, work to build a stronger connection between the mind and the body. Emotions also activate a physical response associated with your brain's reward core. Such unconscious comparisons will take time to break down after years of responding to a particular situation or feeling by using them. It can help you learn what real emotions you encounter when you are stimulated. Practices such as yoga, meditation, and breathing exercises can put you in more contact with your body, helping you feel triggers as they come. Methods such as these can also serve as positive tools to help you overcome triggers without using your mind and body to calm down. While counting to five as you inhale and exhale, something as simple as taking long, deep breaths can trigger your nervous system to start calming you down when hit by a craving. These crucial few seconds of mind-body awareness help you to overcome your needs and more recent ones.

Second, learn some valuable coping skills to help get you into emotional distress across moments. Holding an object like a "worry stone" to rub between your fingertips when you feel anxious is an example of a sensory-based strategy for relaxing your mind and body. Other procedures like getting up and walking, listening to music, coloring, hitting a punching bag, or playing with a pet can help you get through emotional triggers without having to use them.

When you stay in good physical health, you'll feel fewer negative feelings, both total and day today. Drinking too much caffeine, skipping meals, waiting too late, and becoming flabby will all transform your overall emotional state into "grumpy and irritable." Consistently follow good health practices — ask your doctor if you're not sure where to start. So give yourself regular breaks, both mentally, and in terms of making choices, so you don't always get it right.

And even if you're feeling pessimistic, make a habit of talking positive — especially in anticipating a happy, sober future!

The support network of friends is another vital resource for recuperation. Going to meetings and getting to know other addicts helps build a robust network of people who can help you deal with your sobriety even in the most challenging moments. If you feel incredibly agitated and your mind starts spinning, it can sometimes mean the difference between using and remaining sober contacting someone who can help you manage and survive the experience.

Finding emotional awareness techniques, mind-body connection, and coping skills that work for you is crucial. Investing in your psychological wellness and social relationships can help you stay on top of the emotional triggers and withstand cravings and awkward moments without using drugs or alcohol.

Positive people do not live in a magical world full of unicorns and rainbows. We also spend a large portion of our time thinking about the challenges of life.

What is the difference between the positive ones and the negative? The difference is not what we think about— it's whether we choose to ruminate over or react productively to our troubles. Each problem in life will sound like a giant boulder to the pessimistic thinking cutting off their path through life. But the challenges of life become an opportunity for optimistic thinking to climb over that boulder and continue along their route!

How do we start recognizing negative thought patterns so we can start changing them? Most common forms of negative patterns of thought include:

• All-or-nothing thinking— You believe a complete failure is anything less than perfection. "If I don't finish my planned Thanksgiving dish, what's even the point of making dinner?"

• Disqualification of positive aspects— You focus on the negative aspects of an experience but fail to recognize that these negative aspects are often intermingled with positive aspects. "I haven't won the race, so it doesn't matter if my time was a personal best."

• Harmful self-labeling — By making negative assumptions about yourself, you respond to adverse circumstances. "Missing the piano recital of my daughter means I am a terrible father."

• Catastrophic — You believe your actions will lead to the worst-case scenario. "I have found a mistake in my CV. Now I will not get that job or any other job, and I will be unemployed forever. "Do either of these patterns of thought look familiar?

When you take a step back to look at these patterns of thinking, you can say that they are unhelpful and unreasonable ways of solving problems. If a friend shared one of these negative thinking habits, you'd probably point out how their reasoning process was flawed— yet, we often don't think we can step back and correct our incorrect thinking patterns!

A proactive thinker might address each of these things with a better answer, such as:

• "Whoops, it looks like I can't finish all I've planned. Keep ingredients for pecan pie for later, and enjoy this evening's pumpkin pie. "

•" Wow, the other competitors were fast today! Yet I ran faster than I ever had before in a meeting, so it looks like I'm getting better! "By missing her piano recital, I let my daughter down. I have to work harder to show her I care about her achievements. I better put her next swim meeting on my calendar and make sure that there's nothing else to plan during that period. "

•" Whoops, there's a mistake on my CV! Perhaps if the HR manager sees this, she will realize that errors are happening. The next person who reads my resume understands that I pay attention to details. "You may have noticed that the optimistic thinkers in these cases still admit that they have made mistakes, but they bounce back quickly with ways to solve their problems in the future.

Just as time spent around negative people can poison our thoughts, mindful habits of spending time around supportive people can help our brains develop positive thinking patterns. These patterns of view help us believe we can overcome the challenges we face. As your brain learns optimistic people's speech and reasoning patterns, you will find your self-talk also becoming more positive.

Much better, you have a whole bunch of friends to pick you up when you feel down on your ability to overcome addiction if you spend time with optimistic people. Recovery is the most difficult challenge, mentally and emotionally, that many people will face in their lives. At some point in your path, you are likely to turn to someone and say, "I don't know if I can do it." You must have people in your life who are going to say, "I care for you, I believe in you, and I know you can." Positive people are often enjoying an active social life. If they enjoy an activity, they make sure that they try it out and frequently practice it. Try to join an organized group like a book club or kickball team, or look at learning new skills by taking a class like drawing or improving. If you find your faith reliable, join a church, synagogue, mosque, or other spiritual community.

Many people who fall into alcohol or drug addiction tend to adopt an extremely negative attitude of mind. The main reason is that the person will have plenty to feel wrong about as addiction takes them in a spiraling downward. The reason addicts get caught in negativity is because they use this to explain their actions. We can be used as an excuse to misuse alcohol and drugs by pointing out all the negative things in life. For this reason, the person also needs to give up their negative outlook on life to escape addiction successfully.

You made mistakes in the past; we all make mistakes. Many choices have more affected your life than others, such as wanting to drink and doing drugs. Nonetheless, you start a new journey when you decide to seek the recovery of drugs and alcohol. Even though you've made mistakes, you have to let them go and forgive yourself before the anger spreads. It's a slippery slope back into addiction after the negative thoughts surface.

Negative thoughts foster a victim's mentality, foster a sense of hopelessness, and prevent you from realizing your potential. We hinder the growth mindset, which is a crucial part of addressing the challenges facing sobriety in the first year.

Here are some examples of negative thoughts that are common during the early recovery stages.

- Assuming there's something "wrong" with you as a person — "I can't get sober because I don't have any willpower."

• Reducing complicated problems to black and white examples— "Therapy didn't work for my uncle when he wanted to stop drinking, so it won't work for me."

• Bitterness about the past— "It's the fault of my ex-wife that I'm drinking. If she hadn't filed for divorce, I wouldn't be an addict. "

• Minimizing your accomplishments—"I've been clean for a week, but that's nothing. I won't be able to keep it that way forever. "

• Harshly judging minor errors —" I'm such an idiot. How will I remain sober if I can't even remember a single appointment for therapy?"

• Feeling as if you don't deserve grace—" I want to be alone forever because of what I did to my friends and family when I was high. "

• Resenting others —" To stay sober is easier for others because their lives are less complicated than mine. "

• Making unfounded judgments about others—" It's pointless to try to find a new job. No one will want to hire someone who has been fired because of an addiction. "At home, the key to stopping negative thoughts is to remember that what you feel isn't necessarily a reflection of what's happening. Talking about the situation in a journal will help you think about your feelings more objectively.

Ask yourself the question of three: • Is this thought real?

• Is that a significant thought?

• Is that a helpful idea?

Another great strategy is committing to treating yourself the same way a close friend would treat you. Could you tell a friend who suffered that it was impossible to improve her condition, or that she deserved having bad things happen to her? Not! Keep in mind that you are deserving of the same love and respect you would give to a friend in need, no matter what has happened in the past.

Although it may not seem like a healthy lifestyle can make a difference in your attitude, making time for exercise, nutritious meals, and enough sleep will help to stabilize your mood. This is particularly true if you go for a positive start to your day, like making time for a calming yoga routine or walking in the park.

Recall the healing is more than just an abstention from addictive drug use. You are setting yourself up a new, wellness-focused life. It involves the regeneration of the mind, body, and spirit.

Chapter 7: Therapies

A category of disorders that can inflict physical and psychological harm is addictive disorders. Treatment is necessary to break the cycle of addiction.

Nevertheless, addiction is difficult to treat as a chronic disease, which needs ongoing care.

It is safe to say that in the "outside of the norm" context, alternative treatments for addiction are no longer, in essence, alternative. Most treatment facilities and clinicians today offer a range of these forms of "supplemental" treatments, like acupuncture, equine (horse) therapy, neurofeedback, biochemical regeneration, hypnotherapy, yoga, watsu (water therapy), meditation, ropes course, sound therapy, and much more.

People can fall into serious addiction from all walks of life, often switching from painkillers to illicit drugs and alcohol. You may be struggling to surmount a prescription drug habit, or fighting heroin or meth addiction. Finding a recovery plan can be difficult that can help you overcome your issues. There is a growing trend in using alternative therapy as a way to resolve drug addiction, and healing sessions alongside addiction therapy, meditation, and sound therapy may be a positive way to overcome your cravings.

Anxiety and stress are primary factors that interfere with the recovery of substance addiction. Sound therapy uses pitch, rhythm, and vibration to bring about beneficial cellular-level changes and relieves stress.

When someone is in addiction recovery from alcohol and other substance use, a perfect way to establish a well-rounded treatment plan is to use a wide variety of skills and techniques.

For many, the introduction of mindfulness-based practices such as addiction recovery therapy will encourage sobriety and overall wellbeing.

7.1 Advice on Meditation

Meditation is an alternative and complementary approach (CAM) to traditional addiction recovery programs, such as psychotherapy and group counseling. By tandem with these, this mind and body exercise will improve the benefits of conventional therapies.

Most people who recover from addiction find that they have lost touch with how their minds and bodies feel, as habit acts as a way to disconnect you from your mind and body.

Meditation is an act designed to connect the mind and body. People have practiced meditation for thousands of years to create a calm, relaxed, and healthy account while improving their physical health. People are now using meditation for many physical and mental conditions, or to improve their overall health.

Meditation today is a collective term often associated with health skills such as stress management, and assists in the healing process of several disease conditions, other commonly known side benefits include improved self-awareness, reduced anxiety, autoimmune stimulation, and increased wellbeing feelings. It was adapted for use in sports training and can increase our level of awareness. It has also been part of an extensive treatment program to aid in the recovery of drugs as a supportive healing process.

Working with meditation is based on a view of the world that there is more to life than to the physical. That we have an emotional and spiritual dimension to our being and that our physical bodies have a subtly integrated structure in it.

This area of energy is as dynamic and multifunctional as our physical body, with all its subsystems and organ systems. When each step of the meditation procedure is integrated into a specific sequence of symbols, shapes, colors, and mandalas, it is possible to repair the damage done to these subtle structures and to stimulate the body to heal.

Meditation accesses the power of inner healing in all humans but often goes unrecognized. Because meditation uses the language of intuition and the unconscious, it is possible to access the more profound and excluded areas of the necessary healing. Fast all the experiences and awareness of altered states accessed when using drugs are distortions of real insight. An analogy may be helpful about what drug abuse does. If we compare the physical and energetic being of the person to a house, the use of drugs will damage the rooms, crush windows, puncture holes through walls, rip off parts of the roof and flooring.

Meditation is a generally safe exercise that focuses on the link between the mind and the body to induce relaxation and serenity. Physical and mental wellbeing is improving.

Meditation with carefulness is also an excellent way to help control mood. It can decrease the levels of the stress hormone cortisol, increase the compound interleukin of the immune system and assist in the capacity of the body to detoxify itself from harmful chemicals, which can affect neurotransmitter receptors and alter the mood.

Meditation need not take place over a given length of time. Beginners should start meditating at a time for a couple of minutes and work up to longer sessions. You don't have to participate in religiously or spiritually.

The practice focuses on the perception of current perceptions, emotions, physical sensations, and surroundings. Attention often means accepting feelings and thoughts as they are without criticizing or marking them.

Though different styles appear different, they may share similar elements, including:

• A calming atmosphere with minimal distractions and interruptions

• A comfortable posture reached by sitting, standing or lying down

• Focused attention to help free the mind from stress, concern, and anxiety

• Calm and relaxed breathing to increase the supply of oxygen in the body

• An open account to embrace thoughts.

The person works in mindfulness meditation to build their awareness of the present situation and the present moment.

Someone who uses conscious meditation will attend to their present experience by noticing the thoughts in their minds and the breath in their bodies. They will observe these sensations without labeling them as "good or bad" or "right or wrong." Someone new to meditation might find a guided, mindful meditation helpful, and an excellent way to get started with a meditation practice. A guide (usually someone skilled in practicing or leading meditation) should direct the person through a mental simulation to tap into the fragrances, tastes, touches, sounds, and sights associated with the imagined environment.

Although meditation techniques may vary, they are all producing beneficial effects. Much better, even after the exercise ends, the positive influence of mindfulness continues.

In general, meditation helps foster a sense of inner peace and calmness, promotes self-awareness, improves mental functioning, and helps the individual detach themselves from thoughts and desires, which can help reduce cravings and avoid relapse.

Meditation can offer multiple psychological and physical benefits to a person in recovery, such as:

• Decreased blood pressure: meditation can improve the blood pressure of those at risk of hypertension;

• Improvement of the immune system: A mindful meditation program can enhance the functioning of the immune system.

• Relief of pain: meditation can decrease subjective pain ratings in individuals who practice it.

• Anxiety relief: meditative techniques can help control anxiety among individuals.

• Stress management: Meditation can yield small to moderate stress improvements.

• Lack of depressive symptoms: Improvement of depression in meditation practitioners.

• Better sleep: Insomniac sleep may be improved by meditation.

There are lots of different meditative exercises. Trying every technique will allow you to choose which one is working best for you.

• Breathe: breathe naturally, concentrating on inhalation and exhalation.

• Progressive relaxation of the muscle: this form of meditation brings awareness to every part of your body and ultimately relaxes from head to toe.

Mantra-based: Loudly or internally repeat a word or phrase. If your mind wanders, put the slogan back to your heart.

• Guided: a trained teacher guides you verbally through the process of meditation.

• Please focus on the movement: this involves physical exercise, such as walking, yoga, biking, and surfing, being conscious of every part of your body as it moves.

What works for one person may not work for another, so if you are interested in trying meditation to suppress cravings and avoid relapse, keeping an open mind when trying new approaches is crucial. Still, as with all other treatment strategies used in this field of work, it cannot be stand-alone and is not intended to replace other therapies. It must be used in combination with other specialist services, in particular, counseling, life-skills re-education, anger management, communication skills, relationship preservation, and in an ideal world, family therapy, and environmental change.

7.2 Addiction and Sound Therapy

Sound therapy is a treatment that is gaining growing use in treating addiction. Sounds are produced in various ways, including the use of gongs, drums, and chimes. The therapy also makes use of digital technology to provide specific frequencies and sound patterns. The goal of sound therapy healing is to use the vibrations created to create change within the mind, which enables the brain to begin healing, to restore the circuitry previously damaged by addiction. It also helps to recreate the impression that you are part of nature, with a sense of security and peace.

While people from different cultures have been using vibrations for successful healing practice for centuries, the effects of music and sound on human emotions have only recently started to be studied by researchers.

This holistic approach is focused on getting the mind into the present moment. It stimulates positive emotions and brain pathways.

It is a useful tool for managing cravings, impulsiveness, and negative mental states. Sound therapy can also be seen as a form of mindfulness, directing consciousness to the present moment. This can be helpful and effective in treating the symptoms and root causes of addiction. It is relieving to the brain that is either craving drugs or trapped in negative emotional situations.

If you have never studied music or looked deeply into this online stuff, essentially a frequency is the rate per second of a sound wave vibration. Such waves of sound are expressed in' hertz' (or Hz). Healing frequencies are then a particular hertz scale that monks supposedly used during meditation in Gregorian times. There are two frequencies with which the body resonates very well, one is 432Hz, and one is 444Hz, so they harmonize our body patterns. There are also some tunings— 396, 417, 528, 639, 741, 852— that do different things. Such frequencies are known as Solfeggio.

Solfeggio frequencies are believed to have been used in sacred music, including the beautiful and well-known Gregorian chants. The chants and their unique tones, when sung in harmony, were believed to impart spiritual blessings. Each sound of the Solfeggio consists of a frequency necessary to adjust your strength and be in perfect harmony with your body, mind, and spirit.

396 Hz–Liberating Guilt and Fear 417 Hz–Undoing Situations and Facilitating Change 528 Hz–Transformation and Miracles (DNA Repair) 639 Hz–Connection / Relationships 741 Hz–Expression / Solutions 852 Hz–Return to Spiritual Order Addiction lives in mind, body, and spirit.

The body is in the earliest stages of recuperation from addiction during treatment — toxic energy lives within joints and muscles, which inhibit complete recovery. Additionally, rapid recovery causes a lot of stress due to withdrawal, coping with emotions, and working through cravings.

Sound therapy helps to neutralize the brain, promote healing in the body, and create a sense of calm that is sorely needed.

Whether these effects are due to physical changes in the body or are merely a placebo effect, those who have been doing sound healing have had significant benefits and a new sense of wholeness.

While sound healing might seem like a new phenomenon, it has been around for centuries, the truth is. In reality, records show vibroacoustic practices of healing date back to ancient cultures that incorporated music into their holistic methods of healing to achieve a state of equilibrium.

Sound Therapy operates with a steady frequency to synchronize our brainwaves, which leads to calm consciousness, meditative state, or even sleep. This position of quietness encourages:

• Slow breath

• Increased awareness

• Released physical stress. In this state, listeners may tap into their "subtle body," which harbors imbalances and traumas, establishing blockages and regions of mind, body, and spirit that need to be resolved for a holistic cure.

Sound calming therapy provides holistic health advantages for many mental and physical conditions such as

• Sleep disorders

• Anxiety

• Depression

• Stress reduction

• PTSD • Pain management

• Substance use disorders Many goals can be accomplished with music therapy intervention, rather than a person resort to drugs or alcohol, including

• More optimistic thoughts and moods

• A sense of congeniality

• Increased capacity to focus and pay attention

• Increased desire and ability to resolve disputes between peers and families Used as part of a comprehensive treatment program combined with conventional, evidence-based treatments, music therapy may help those suffering from addictions.

7.3 Emotional Sobriety: The Key to Addiction Recovery

The secret to addiction lies in emotional patterns. Such habits rage on us, without us knowing it until we reach a point where almost everything triggers the same response— fear, grief, or anger. Overwhelmed by these emotions, we are seeking relief— which wouldn't— in some act or substance that can confuse, divert, or deaden our feelings. The thing is, this "solution" isn't one. This fixes the symptoms, but the underlying cause is not. Our emotions continue to flood, and we grow ever more reliant on our answer to the point of being obsessed with it.

Emotions are incredibly durable. Your feelings expand your capacity for productivity, self-care, and healthy relationships if properly managed and integrated with cognitive functions like logic and reason. Since emotions developed as primitive instincts, reasoning, and logical considerations can be bypassed, sometimes leading us to disregard consequences. That is precisely what they feel when someone has an emotional addiction.

Once emotions are idolatrous over healthy coping skills, the addiction established can lead a person to experience adverse side effects such as

• Unwise decision-making

• Inappropriate behaviors

• Faulty self-management or planning

• Impaired productivity

• Injured relationships

• When someone is reliant on stress relief emotions, they are likely to turn to other self-medicating sources

• Another way of looking at emotional dependency is as a nervous habit. Habit formation happens when repetitive actions become second nature. So forming an edgy pattern involves unconsciously preparing yourself to respond with a default emotional reaction to a variety of triggers. With time, that feeling becomes a basis for how you react to the world. When rage is your default emotion, you can find that you turn to it whenever you're unsure. You may even feel calm, as this emotion is washing over you.

Mental wellbeing is a crucial factor, too, in the same way, that physical fitness plays a significant role in recovery. Being emotionally healthy goes beyond mere happiness; instead, the idea of emotional wellbeing requires the practice of paying attention to emotions, feelings, moods, and actions, whether positive or negative. Ultimately, being unhappy in a suitable situation (for example, when receiving lousy news) can be an informative, adaptive response; acceptance of emotional health unhappiness is a normal, natural (and even healthy) reaction to bad press and understanding that sadness will pass in time.

Recovery from drug or alcohol addiction is more than just becoming abstinent.

A detox may help you get away from active addiction, but what's stopping you from returning to it or trading one addiction for another? The key to that is emotional sobriety. Because there is no proven cure for addiction, this is the thing that will most definitely give you healthy and permanent sobriety.

Emotional sobriety essentially means maintaining a healthy and responsible lifestyle consisting of the following elements:

- Being able to manage feelings and mood

- Maintaining a rational outlook on conditions

- Being flexible/able to cope even when things get difficult

- Recognition and management of negative thoughts and behaviors

- Maintaining at the moment and not overthinking the past or the Powerful future feelings should in most cases be handled appropriately. Distraction or repression, however, is likewise natural reactions.

While these can be normal even for a healthy mind in extreme situations, they should not be so in the case of minor stresses on life. During early recovery, they are also familiar with people before they practice emotional sobriety.

Where mental sobriety is all about self-regulation and equilibrium, the reverse is addiction. That is the lack of self-control. The first step in healing is abstinence or physical sobriety. The second step is to try out relational sobriety, and ideally maintain it. This can mostly be seen as detoxification and therapy, which are at the heart of most treatments for addiction recovery.

Addiction is a chronic illness that has no known cure. While abstinence will help you eradicate addiction from your life, emotional sobriety helps free you from addiction in your life. It is necessary if long-lasting recovery is to be guaranteed.

If you're not dealing with your underlying problem and learning to regulate your emotions, you may find that even if you're in recovery, you're suffering from being a' dry drunk.'

Awareness is not only counseling but also one of the best skills to learn to maintain mental sobriety. Yoga and meditation are often recommended as support, but you can also take courses in mindfulness. Meanwhile, try to put some of this into your life: Feel What You Feel Emotional Sobriety is all about acceptance, and allow yourself to feel what your body wants to feel. If you're upset, then accept that you're angry and then understand why. You'll only be able to deal with it by finding where the problem lies.

Stop and Think. Now, having identified the problem, is it worth getting this upset about? If so, find a healthy way to wind up, then consider potential solutions so that you can solve it ASAP. If no, give yourself a bit of permission to become frustrated, then find a way to move on.

It is not always that easy, of course. Surely, you know how much it "helps" when you're screaming, and someone is telling you, "Calm down," or when you're down, and someone's giving the suggestion, "Cheer up! "Doesn't it make you feel better? That's why it's essential to be able to identify and articulate your emotions and be able to address them. That's a talent, though, that could take time to learn.

Don't dwell. It's normal to be overcome with memories or future worries. But concentrating on the here and now is much healthier for your mental health. You cannot change what's happened, and you can't predict what's going to happen.

That is especially important when dealing with new issues. Although learning from past mistakes and anticipating future consequences is wise, dwelling on either one for too long will bring little progress. For a healthy recovery, self-forgiveness is crucial.

Help Is Important Social interactions and general support for preserving emotional sobriety is essential. It doesn't mean you need lots of friends, but you're expected to shape meaningful connections. That way, you communicate with people all the time, which is essential when learning to convey and cope with emotions — finding someone to reach out to always helps.

Reappraisal of transition polarity is an essential aspect of mental sobriety. This applies to be able to confront and change a negative situation into a positive one. Such as if you lost your job, you now have a chance to work in a better place or try a new career. A circumstance you might not be able to change, but you may be able to change your mind and approach.

Emotional wellbeing is a critical factor in encouraging overall health and recuperation. In the present day, being able to put past events into perspective creates contentment and balance, and pave the way for a sane future. When it comes to substance use and mental health issues, relapse triggers and other recovery challenges may commonly be encountered; however, maintaining emotional wellness helps us to equip ourselves with the tools and ideas needed to correct the recovery path and promote long-term health.

Chapter 8: The Disease of Suffering and the Medicine of the Noble Path

The Buddha is likened to a doctor because he was concerned with the pain that ails us all. The Buddha is also called The Great Healer. He is the only physician who supplies medication for the treatment of human disease.

Buddha taught the "cure" of suffering illness, not by trying to rule us with "can't" dos— but by educating us about what we can do.

The essence of the teaching of the Buddha can be summarized in two principles: The Four Noble Truths and the Noble Eightfold Path. The first covers the doctrinal side, and the primary response it elicits is understanding; the second covers the training side, in the broadest sense of that word, and the fundamental answer it calls for is action.

The Four Noble Truths, the central tenet of Buddhism, can mostly be summed up as follows: 1. There is sacrifice; 2. The cause of misery is greed for selfishness and ignorance; 3. There is a way to bring the pain to an end, and 4. The Noble Eightfold Path will bring the pain to an end.

A person who does not surmount his worldly desires, according to the Buddha, is doomed to repeat his miserable life through an endless cycle of death and rebirth— a condition known as samsara.

Nevertheless, once that person reaches enlightenment — that is, he truly knows the cause of his misery, and sweeps away all material attachments— he ends his process and enters nirvana, which is the state of enlightenment and true happiness.

The ugly truth which can be gleaned from the teaching of Buddha for people suffering from addiction is this: If they put an end to their appetite for alcohol or drugs, they can begin their process of misery toward destruction.

The guide to the end of suffering is found within the fourth noble truth: the noble eightfold path. The eight parts of the liberation path are grouped into three essential elements of Buddhist practice — moral behavior, mental discipline, and wisdom; In virtually all of his discourses, the Buddha taught the eightfold path and his directions are as clear and practical to his followers today as they were when he first gave them.

The Buddha understood problems with addiction and consequently cautioned his disciples, but this was not the primary focus of his teachings.

Having long-standing Buddhist traditions, Thailand and Japan have developed Buddhist influenced responses to addiction. Buddhism, with its focus on desire and connection, an awareness of the workings of the mind, and the ways to work with your account, lends itself as a productive tool to help recover addiction. The 12-step movement was an impetus to make use of Buddhist ideas and practices. Consciousness, in particular, has started to be used to promote addiction treatment, with promising results. Exploring other aspects of Buddhism is beginning and may bring additional benefits in the future.

8.1 The Noble Eightfold Path-A Guide towards Recovery

While referred to as steps on a path, the eightfold approach is not intended as a linear learning process but as eight aspects of life, all of which must be incorporated into everyday life. You are certainly also aware of the moral codes in other religious groups, including Judaism, Jews, and Muslims.

While a degree of continuity does exist across these classes, each theory has different interpretations of the code. The eightfold path in Buddhism is meant as a guideline to be considered, contemplated, and only when each step is entirely accepted as part of life you are seeking. Buddhism never calls for blind faith; it aims to encourage learning and a self-discovery process.

The Eightfold Path to the Noble is

1. Right Consciousness

2. Right goal /

3. Right, Speak

4. Fair Action

5. Living Right

6. Right Strength

7. Purposefulness

8. Right Concentration

Buddha emphasized to put all human behavior within one of eight categories or directions. Each path referred to by the term "right," which means ethical or moral. He then defined the behavioral styles that were appropriate for each of those groups.

The eightfold path has three main groups: two wisdom paths (how we understand), three conduct paths (how we act), and three concentration paths (how we think).

"Right View" and "Right Intention" are the two paths of wisdom. "Right View" is sometimes called "right understanding." It means seeing things are they are, which means seeing them objectively and thoroughly and understanding them fully. It needs accurate observation and analysis to follow. In other terms, we will discuss what we have learned. Only then can we have "true understanding." "True Intention" is sometimes called "right thought," meaning we don't have to see it through the negative emotion prism. We must free ourselves from greed, covetousness, hate, anger, and other negative emotions that may cloud our judgment. Only then can we have "right thinking." The three paths of behavior are: "right speech" means we have to have respect for the truth. We are not supposed to lie; we are not supposed to slander; we are not supposed to gossip; we are not supposed to speak ill of others. We have to avoid harsh or cruel expressions that cause harm or quarrels. Essentially, if we talk, it means treating others with respect and considering the consequences of our words.

"Right Action" means being who respects all life and who maintains good relations with others. We shouldn't kill any living thing on purpose, not even a mosquito. We should not steal from them. (Stealing means we should not take anything that is not given freely; it does not entail defrauding or tricking anyone.) We should not "use" other people to our advantage. We shouldn't indulge in adultery or sexual misconduct.

Right action means living by all other forms of teachings of the Buddha.

"Right Livelihood" is a "right practice" extension, but the emphasis is on how we earn our living. We should not do any work involving killing (including the slaughtering of animals) or dealing with slaves, firearms, poisons, or intoxicants (drugs or alcohol).

Three concentration paths are: "Right Effort" means maintaining a positive attitude and approaching tasks with enthusiasm and cheerful resolve. In our job, we have to avoid becoming too intense, but also avoid slacking out.

It also means avoiding mischievous feelings. To the subconscious, it's "right action."

"Right mindfulness" means that as we go through our day, we should be conscious and focused. We should avoid distracted or confused mentality. This means being able to concentrate with a calm mind on the task at hand without our mind wandering off or getting intruding worries.

It's not meditation, but it asks us to be aware of what we do physically and mentally. It means being conscious of what we are doing, what we hear, and what we are talking about.

Did you ever drive, and suddenly realize you're at your exit and you don't know how you got there? The monotony of driving on the highway can cause us to lose conscience. Another example is eating in front of your television. Have you ever done this and found unexpectedly that your plate is bare, but you don't want to eat? Eating carefully is essential for good health.

"Righteous Meditation" means meditation. This creates inner tranquility, and at the same time, sharpens awareness. It is hard to do right, and faithful practice is needed. To achieve total stillness of mind and body, it requires "emptying the mind."

The Buddha was aware of the problems caused by addictive behavior, especially drinking and gambling, and gave his followers advice to help. However, his primary focus was to help people achieve enlightenment, as he did, characterized by wisdom and compassion. The insight side of knowledge requires a detailed understanding of the mind's workings, as well as actions that will help move towards enlightenment.

The Buddha described desire and attachment as the principal cause of suffering. Addiction can be described as a sort of severe attachment. The driving force behind that is the human desire to avoid pain and enjoyment. When people can conquer their connection, then it will help them to break their addiction. That means the Buddha's center of the teachings gives a path away from alcohol or drug abuse for followers.

1. **Right, Understanding**. Right Understanding or right view is the first step on the eightfold path.

The understanding of things as they are is right, and it is the four noble truths that explain things as they are. In the end, therefore, correct understanding is limited to the interpretation of the four noble truths. This perception is the ultimate awareness that shows the Absolute Truth. There are two sorts of knowledge, according to Buddhism. What we commonly call "comprehension" is knowledge, an accumulated memory, an intellectual grasp of a subject according to specific data. This is called "Understanding Now." It is not very insightful. Real deep understanding or "penetration" is seeing a thing, without name and label, in its true nature. This penetration is only possible when the mind is free of all impurities and develops fully through meditation.

We come to know that cause and effect rule everything. The four truths are eternal nature. We gain insight into this phase about the impermanent, unsatisfactory, and impersonal quality of life. Forgiveness can and is essential.

Buddha means seeing things from the right perspective, in the right way. To see things as they are, with no false expectations or pretensions. He wanted his followers to see and understand the transitory nature of worldly ideas and possessions, and to understand that only if they practiced the right karma can they attain salvation.

This is a significant step along the path as it relates to seeing the world and everything in it as it is, not as we think it is or wants it to be. Just as you can read the directions on a map and then make the journey, it is essential to study, translate, and review the details but only to plan for the trip. So direct personal experience will bring us to a more profound level of Right Understanding.

Knowing reality is of very little value in our lives if we don't put it to personal use.

2. **Right Intent**. A Right Purpose is the second step on the Eightfold Path. This is the step in which we get engaged on the path. Right understanding shows us what life is, and what the problems of life are made up of, Right Intent urges us to decide what our heart wants.

Buddha says it is because of what we think that we are what we are. Our course of action is dictated by what is going on within our minds (our thought process). Therefore it is necessary to follow the direction of Right Thought or Right Intention. An individual should be aware of his intention or role in life and is studying Buddha's teachings, having the right Intent or the right thought.

Right thinking signifies the feelings of selfless renunciation or alienation, loving thoughts, and non-violent thoughts that are extended to all beings. It is exciting and vital to note here that views on the side of wisdom are grouped by selfless detachment, compassion, and nonviolence. It clearly shows that real knowledge is filled with these noble qualities and that all thoughts of selfish desire, ill-will, hate, and violence result from a lack of wisdom in all spheres of life, whether human, social, or political.

We are renouncing greed, hate, and delusion. With unattached appreciation, we train our minds to meet all pain with compassion, and all pleasure. We cultivate generous, compassionate, and kind wishes for all living beings. We practice modesty and sincerity, and we live with dignity.

The real purpose must come from the heart and requires, beginning with yourself, respecting the dignity of all life and consideration for all that exists.

Right Intent means to love and dedication for the journey. Setting up to climb a high mountain means you have to consider the lay of the land, the dangers, the other members of the team, and the equipment you need. That is close to the definition of right. But if you want to climb and have a passion for climbing, you'll only climb the mountain. This is meant correctly. Our journey through life is the mountain that we climb here.

In summary, knowing correctly will eradicate ignorance. We then eliminate desire with the Right Intent and right understanding, which in turn causes the suffering described in the Four Noble Truths.

3. Right Speech. Right Speech is The Path's next step. We continue to undervalue the influence of the spoken word, and often express words of regret in haste. Each of us has endured the frustration of harsh criticism, warranted or not, and we are also likely to have felt good when kind words have inspired us.

Buddha asks his followers to speak the truth, to avoid slander and gossip, and to refrain from the language of abuse. It is also necessary to avoid harsh words that can cause distress or offend others while also staying clear of meaningless idle chatter that lacks any meaning.

In the community, we take refuge as a place to practice wise communication and support others on their paths. In our interactions, we practice being frank, knowledgeable, and patient, asking the community for help and allowing others to direct us through the process. Over the challenges and achievements we encounter, we cultivate transparency, integrity, and modesty.

Right speech involves acknowledging the truth, as well as being aware of the impact of idle gossip and repeating rumors. Thoughtfully communicating helps unite others, and can heal dissension. Through deciding never to talk unkindly, or in frustration, a spirit of empathy emerges that brings us closer to the compassionate everyday life.

4. Right Action. Right Action acknowledges the importance of taking the ethical approach in life, respecting others, and the world in which we work. It involves not making what is not offered to us and upholding the agreements we sign in both our private and business lives.

Right Action also covers the Buddha's five precepts not to kill, steal, cheat, resist sexual misconduct, and not take drugs or other intoxicants.

Each move on the road also involves a whole approach to the climate, with Right Action being taken to preserve the planet for future generations whenever possible.

Right Action is designed to promote spiritual, noble, and peaceful behavior. This advises us to abstain from destroying life, from cheating, from unethical practices, from illicit sexual intercourse, and to encourage others to live a happy and honorable life in the right way as well.

Behave respectfully and in harmony; Right Action, according to the Buddha, lies in accordance to the following guidelines:- Staying in concert with fellow human beings — Behaving calmly— not cheating— not harming anybody— preventing undue indulgence of sensual pleasure— abstaining from sexual misconduct— not indulging in fraudulent practices, lying and theft We purify our behavior, let us clean our acts. Renunciation of abuse, dishonesty, sexual misconduct, and addiction is the minimum commitment required for the path to recovery and freedom. Our guiding principles are humility, unattached gratitude, empathy, goodness, fairness, dignity, and service.

5. Right Living. The next one on the Eightfold Path follows from Right Action, and this is Right Living. If your research has a lack of respect for life, then moving on the spiritual path will be an obstacle. Buddhism embraces the principle of equality and respect for all living beings.

The Buddha prohibited other types of work, especially those where you deal with harmful drugs and intoxicants, those dealing with weapons, and those harmful to animal or human life. And it would not be recommended for a committed Buddhist to have a liquor store, own a gun shop, or be a butcher. He also opposed the slave trade in his day, which dealt with in human laborers.

And he was also against the tradition of telling fortune as this made predictions of a predetermined future, where his teaching stresses that what we do now determines the future.

Right Livelihood also means that a Buddhist who can, should do some work, either as part of a Buddhist congregation, or in the workplace, or, preferably, do home-based or community service. Most monk communities ensure every member has daily chores, which reminds him of this phase on the Eightfold Path.

Right living means that one should refrain from living through a career that hurts others, such as guns and lethal weapons dealing, intoxicating drinks or poisons, killing animals, stealing, etc., and live by a profession that is noble, blameless, and innocent of harming anyone. One can see here that Buddhism is strongly opposed to any kind of war when it stipulates that arms trade and lethal weapons are an evil and unjust way of living.

In establishing this rule, Buddha encourages his followers to righteously receive their bread and butter, without resorting to immoral and unethical practices. He does not allow his followers to abuse or trade-in weapons or intoxicants, other human beings, or livestock.

If possible, we seek to be of benefit to others, using our time, energy, and resources to help create positive change. We are working towards securing an income/livelihood source that will not cause harm.

6. Right Effort. Right Effort means maintaining an excitement, a healthy, positive attitude. The effort should not be too nervous or too anxious, as should the strings of a musical instrument, nor too slack or too laid back. The right effort should produce a steady, cheerful attitude of determination.

Transparent and honest thoughts should be welcomed to produce Right Effort, and feelings of jealousy and wrath left behind. The right effort is equivalent to positive thinking, and focused Action followed.

On this one, the Buddha was well ahead of his time, and many books were written about the influence of the right attitude.

The right effort is the energetic will to prevent evil and unhealthy states of mind from emerging and to get rid of such evil and unhealthy states that have already arisen within a man, and also to create, to cause tasty and healthy states of mind that have not yet occurred, and to improve and perfect the excellent and wholesome states of mind that are already present in a man.

The Buddha believed that human nature sometimes imposes undue constraints on the mind, causing a person to harbor ill thoughts. So if we want to become better human beings, we have to train our minds to think in the right direction. Once we have gained control of our emotions and replaced the negative with positive ones, we will move in the right direction.

We are committed to the everyday structured practices of meditation, yoga, exercise, wise acts, empathy, grace, humility, compassion, gratitude, and moment-to-moment knowledge of feelings, desires, thoughts, and sensations. The skillful way to know how to apply the right meditation or Action to the given circumstance is formed through effort and energy.

7. Right Mindfulness. While Right Effort is a straightforward concept for most of us, it is somewhat trickier to understand Right Mindfulness and may require quite a change in thought.

I suggest you take a short break, get up and walk around the room or the house (or cruise if you're mobile), and then come back here before reading on.

Right Mindfulness means being conscious of the moment and focused at that moment. As we drive somewhere, we hear noises, see houses, trees, advertise, feel the wind, think about those we left behind, and think about our destination. So it's with most life moments.

Right, Mindfulness asks us to be at that moment mindful of the path and to be at that moment calm and undistracted. Right, Mindfulness is intimately connected with meditation and forms the basis of meditation.

Right, Mindfulness isn't an effort to exclude the universe, the contrary. Right Mindfulness demands that we are aware of the moment, and at that moment, of our actions. We can see how old patterns and behaviors influence us by being conscious. In this knowledge, we may see how fears of possible futures constrain our present actions.

Right awareness is to be always conscious, vigilant, and sensitive to body movements, sensations or emotions, mind and ideas behaviors, perceptions, expectations, and stuff.

Together with the Right Concentration, the right Mindfulness forms the basis of Buddhist meditation. By proposing this, Buddha suggests that his followers mentally focus on their emotions, mental faculties, and abilities while staying away from worldly desires and other distractions.

It refers to the mind's ability to see things as they are without being led astray by greed, avarice, wrath, and ignorance.

We develop wisdom by meditating on formal Mindfulness. It leads to a clear vision and healing of the root causes and conditions which contribute to the addiction suffering. In all aspects of our life, we cultivate present-day knowledge. We are taking refuge at the moment.

Now, having read this, attempt the same walk as before but with a concentrated mind that now focuses solely on the walking motion. Watch your reflections before you move on.

You may get lost occasionally in what you're doing. Those moments can cause music, art, sport. Have you ever done anything with that activity, where your mind is only? You are conscious at that moment, and the Buddha has shown how to incorporate the knowledge into our daily lives.

8. Right Concentration.

When the mind is uncluttered, it can focus on doing anything that is needed. Right attention allows the mind to focus on an object, like a flower or a lit candle, or an idea like loving compassion. That forms the next part of the process of meditation.

Right concentration means that we choose worthy directions for mental strength, though everything in nature, beautiful and wrong, may be useful for attention. Some objects or ideas may be required for further creation at the deeper levels.

The advantages of right Mindfulness and right concentration are essential insofar as they enable the mind to see things, not to see them as we are conditioned, but as they are. These also contribute to a sense of calm and harmony with the world, at the same time. A sense of joy at the moment is felt by being in the moment, and being able to concentrate effectively. Releasing ourselves from the control of past pains and future mind games brings us closer to freeing ourselves from suffering.

Breathing relaxation practice is one of the well-known techniques for mental development, linked with the body. To the body as modes of meditation, there are several other forms of cultivating attentiveness.

We develop the ability to focus the mind on a single object, such as the breath or a phrase, to train the brain through the loving-kindness, compassion, and forgiveness practices to focus on the positive qualities that we seek to uncover. In times of temptation or craving, we use concentration to abstain from acting unwisely.

If you want to go the eightfold path, the most important thing to remember is to be ethical in speech, deed, and thinking. Be a person of good, kind, positive, and moral character. Banish negativity and focus on every activity you do.

With that, you'll be happier and more productive. The eightfold path may not be the most traveled, but it's the one most likely to get you to where you'd like to go.

When a knowledgeable physician treats a patient for a severe illness, his medication is not only for physical care but psychological too. The Noble Eightfold Path, the Path to the End of Sorrow, is a holistic therapy designed to heal through the cultivation of spiritual speech and action, the mental development, and the full progression of one's comprehension and quality of mind. This shows the way to achieve spiritual maturity and to be fully released from suffering.

8.2 How to practice it in a modern age

The Noble Eightfold path has relevance to the present day. Timeless wisdom that can guide the student, parent, or senior of the twenty-first century with the sensible direction that it gave to ancient Buddhist practices.

No matter who you are, the teachings of the Buddha resonate with a reality that reaches each of us actively because it has to do with the road that leads each of us — the path to relieve our suffering and achieve real and enduring peace and happiness.

For this reason, whether you are Buddhist, secular, agnostic, or merely interested in improving yourself, the teachings of the Buddha and his long legacy of 2,500 years are something that can show you how to live more genuinely and honestly.

To provide a summary, the Eightfold Path advises us to practice right speech (not lying or using offensive words), right resolve (being benevolent to all living beings and therefore being a vegetarian is part of being Buddhist), right action (not stealing, killing, committing adultery), right life (possessing what is only required, not harming others, not using/selling animals for meat or weapons)

The Noble Eightfold Path's eternal insight transforms our hearts, welcoming tired travelers to enhanced wellness. So when life is at a standstill and depression and anxiety surface, remember right awareness, right-mindedness, proper voice, right action, right Livelihood, right commitment, right Mindfulness, and right concentration. We will direct our modern life with those basics of wellness. These noble pursuits serve as beacons to spa explorations and bringing the explorer to a more pleasurable destination.

It is a road, one that at any point, need not be perfect. Approach it as the areas for improvement that allow us to relieve our suffering and realize true peace and happiness when taken together as one body.

Do know that, because they are so closely interrelated, you naturally progress in other areas too when you focus on one part of the road.

Operating on Right View, among others, means enhancing Right Thinking and Right Behavior. And practicing Right Mindfulness means nurturing every other place along the path.

For each point on the road, this is valid, so select an area you want to work on first based on how you answered the questions "How am I doing in this?" and "How can I work on improving in this? "And thence step forward with trust.

What are your world-views? Should you hold to your opinions? Knowing the Three Marks of Existence and the Four Noble Truths will allow you to see yourself and the world in the right way.

Our thoughts, words, and actions are all intentionally driven. For instance, when our intentions stem from anger, fear, resentment, or greed, our thoughts, words, and actions are more likely to harm. One great way to learn is by asking ourselves questions about intention, such as:

Why do I think so?

Why did that cause me to tell my spouse?

Which made me so angry that I could throw the remote?

Once you are aware of your intentions, trying to set new ones and replace the old plans is easier.

Lying, chattering, and hurting other people's feelings is not proper speech. It includes all forms of communication (address, voice, email, writing, etc.). This doesn't mean suppressing thoughts or ideas; it means we are aware of the communication's purpose to determine if what we're going to say will do more good or more harm.

The correct expression will decide what I say to someone when I speak to them. Right Mindfulness will keep me from checking my phone when I talk to someone personally.

The 4 Noble Truths and 8-Fold Path of the Buddha were formed for all beings with great love and compassion, and it is in that spirit that I give you the path as well.

Not being Buddhist or not (whether you're interested in that or not), but rather taking your life into your hands and thinking it's too important to live idly.

The path doesn't require you to believe anything else-worldly or extraterrestrial or even require you to give up your present life as it is, it only requires you to think that there is a way out of misery and a path to follow the way to get there diligently.

A journey to a place of greater harmony, prosperity, and patience that transcends the daily challenges and difficulties.

9: Conclusion

Most people say that addiction is an option, but science says otherwise. Sure, getting involved in substance abuse is a choice— at first. Substance abuse is the use of drugs or alcohol in a way that causes problems in your life. Such issues may include your relationships, your finances, or your health. This may be due to legal matters or chances you wouldn't take otherwise, such as unprotected sex.

One of the questions addicted family members sometimes pose is, "Why did this happen? "What is the source of addiction," in other words," According to the National Institute on Drug Abuse, people start to take narcotics for a variety of reasons, including o feel-good — feeling happy," hot "o brushing better— e.g., relieving tension o performing better-improving performance or interest and peer pressure Addiction is a complicated disorder, a brain disease that is characterized through compulsive usage amid harmful consequences. People with addiction (severe substance use disorder) focus heavily on using a particular substance(s), such as alcohol or drugs, to the point where it takes over their lives. We continue to use alcohol or a drug even if we know that it will cause problems. Yet several effective treatments can help people recover from addiction and lead healthy, productive lives.

Active addictions therapies are available.

Recognition of the problem is the first step on the road to recovery. The process of recovery can be hindered if a person denies having a problem and lacks an understanding of substance abuse and addiction. Treatment is often prompted by the intervention of concerned friends and family.

Because addiction affects many aspects of a person's life, they often require multiple types of treatment. For the most part, it is most beneficial to combine medicine with a person or group therapy. Treatment strategies that address the situation of a patient and any medical, psychological, and social issues that co-occur can result in sustained recovery.

Addiction is a condition that is recurrent and often persistent. This usually accompanies many emotional problems. Yet people, mostly on their own, can and do recover from addiction. Individuals will heal, if not on their own, with the aid of their social network or a care provider. Recovery from addiction usually requires numerous attempts. This can lead to feelings of anger and helplessness. Smoking is often seen as one of the most robust forms of addiction to change.

Yet the vast majority of the smokers who have avoided quitting themselves! With the help of professional treatment, others stopped smoking. It's important to remember that many attempts are often needed in the process of overcoming an addiction. Each attempt provides a valuable learning opportunity that changes the experience and moves to get people back closer to their goals despite the difficulties. There are many routes to addiction and many roads to rehabilitation. Consider about addiction recovery as a five-year cycle that will have its ups and downs; after some five years, life will and will be very different. Addiction loses its power as life becomes more worth living.

Addiction is accidental. Associating an addictive behavior of an individual to his moral standards or character may not be rational. The brain reacts to an addict shifts in such a way that despite knowing its dangerous consequences, he continues to live with the bad habits and addictions. In addition to counseling and medications, the person needs lots of love, encouragement, support, and inspiration to get over with the addiction.

Not only is drug or alcohol addiction a matter of concern, but other addictions like gambling, television, social media, video games are also gaining popularity in the addiction sense.

It is essential for the sake of our health that we don't entrust the remote control of our lives to the virtual machine world. The prices are high, and the risks are too many. The young people are learning from our behavior. If they see us being addicted to such video games addiction, the chances are high that they will follow the same path.

We'll have to understand that there's social media for a specific reason. It is suitable for networking and interacting with friends from long distances and with business relations. What's more, a compulsive need to be online all the time, unable to find meaning in real life by remaining active online are specific issues that are red flags. For a better mental, physical, and social health, recognizing the computer addiction that spreads like a sweet poison in society is very crucial.

The future of our society is our young ones. The last thing we need is to see them slip into that dark pit of drug addiction. As adults, we will avoid these cases with the aid of open communication, awareness, and a positive mindset. Nonetheless, there should be no need to feel ashamed and helpless in the event of drug abuse. Delaying the treatment aggravates the case. Once the causes responsible for Facebook addiction come to the fore, one should try to work and healthily solve those problems. Facebook addiction is just a reflection of other more profound and hidden issues in our minds that need to be addressed. Caring for one's mental and physical health should be our top priority for us all. So breaking out of the Facebook addiction would be a significant milestone in that process.

A culture where most adults and teenagers get into the trap of porn addiction becomes an apparent concern for their health.

Watching pornography not only wastes time in a very destructive way, but it also desensitizes the mass and draws it into sexually aggressive and violent acts that could harm other genders or even children. Pornography addiction is a common problem and needs our attention. The only way out is to deal with it in a non-judgmental manner and with patience.

Psychological therapies work well in the drug addict's minds and help the youth gradually to create more self-confidence. Families of those young people who are addicted to drugs should be well aware of the signs of withdrawal so that they are trained from before themselves and know how to handle those circumstances. Strict steps should be taken for a young and healthy society to monitor and eradicate the supply and transactions of such harmful elements. Specific measures must be taken to discourage the young from having access to these medicines of any kind.

It's a road to follow for the rest of our lives— but at every moment, we have the tools at our disposal, if we can note that we're plenty. This moment will suffice if we open our eyes to it only. We know we can make better choices, and through a difficult time, we can help our loved ones. We have the power to get our lives under control, sit with the frustration that happens, accept our suffering, and take care of our feelings rather than blocking out this moment's experience. It is uncomfortable at times; it's hard at times. But there is no way out except by going slowly, one step at a time, firmly rooted in the now.

10: References

KetoGenic Accelerator – (CB) – Venture Supplements. (2020). Retrieved from **https://www.washingtonregion.net/full-text-of-new-testimonial/**

Addictive disorders: Causes and reasons they may get worse. (2020). Retrieved from **https://www.medicalnewstoday.com/articles/323483.php**

Addiction | Psychology Today. (2020). Retrieved from **https://www.psychologytoday.com/us/basics/addiction**

Publishing, H. (2020). How addiction hijacks the brain - Harvard Health. Retrieved from **https://www.health.harvard.edu/newsletter_article/how-addiction-hijacks-the-brain**

Definition of Idiopathic. (2020). Retrieved from **https://www.medicinenet.com/script/main/art.asp?articlekey=3892**

Loneliness and Addiction: Why Do Addicts Isolate Themselves? (2020). Retrieved from **https://www.gatewayfoundation.org/addiction-blog/loneliness-and-addiction/**

McGee, M. (2020). Is Narcissism an Addiction. Retrieved from **https://wellmind.com/2017/07/is-narcissism-and-addiction/**

The Root of Addiction. (2020). Retrieved from **https://www.narcononnewliferetreat.org/addiction-recovery/the-root-of-addiction.html**